Buddhist Heritage
of
Odisha

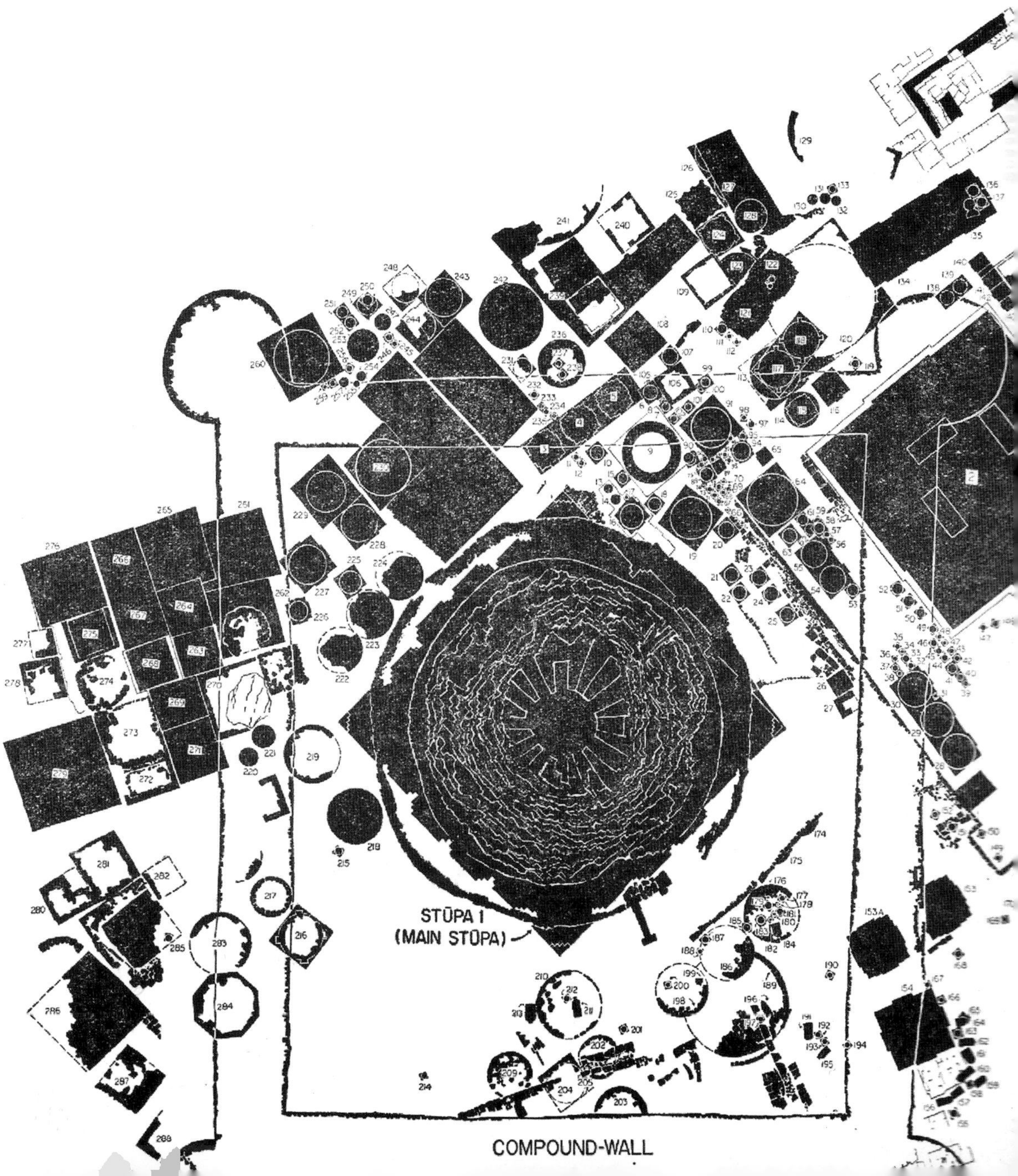

Buddhist Heritage
of
Odisha

Himanshu Prabha Ray

National Monuments Authority
New Delhi

Aryan Books International
New Delhi

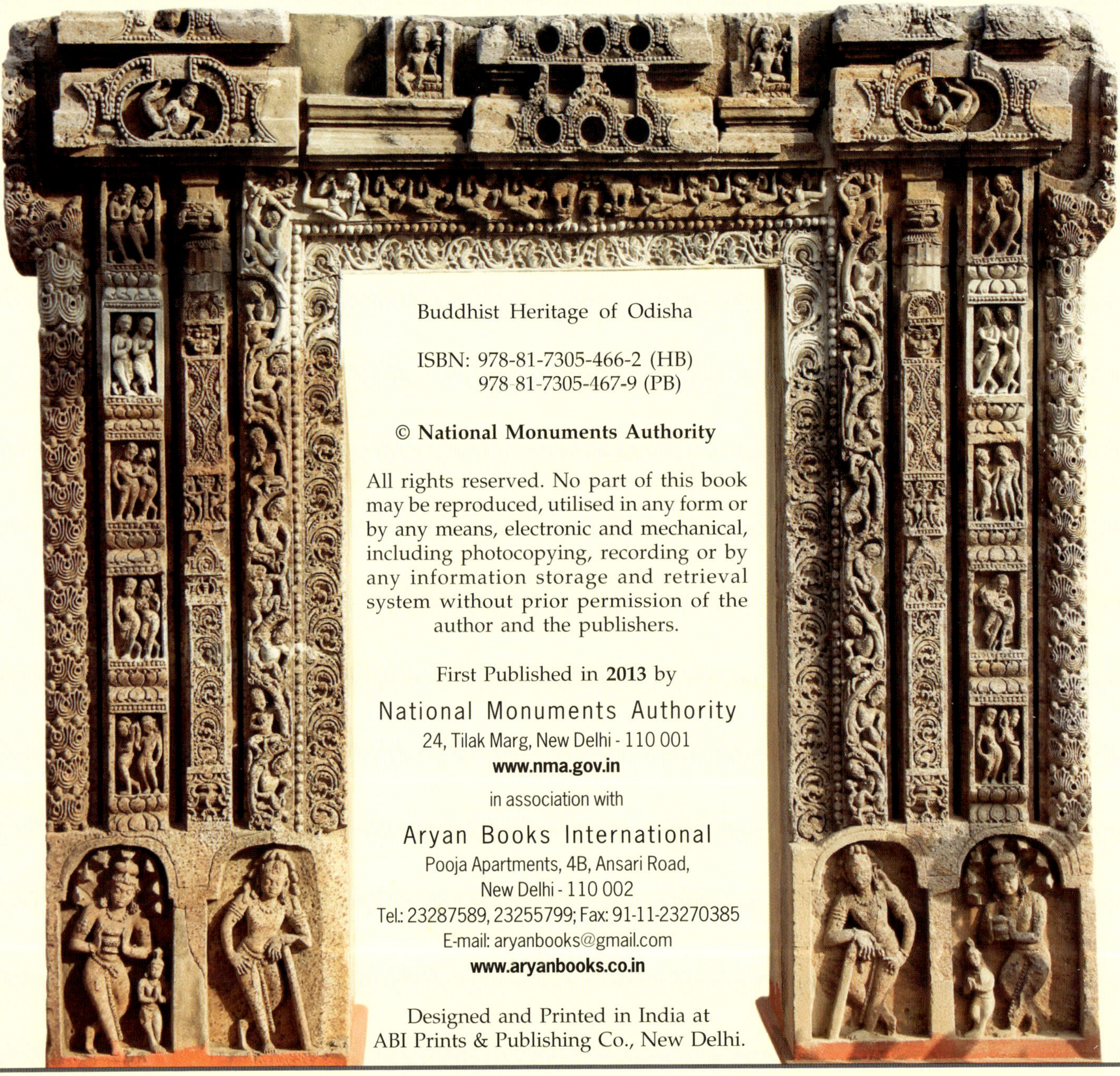

Buddhist Heritage of Odisha

ISBN: 978-81-7305-466-2 (HB)
978-81-7305-467-9 (PB)

First Published in **2013** by

National Monuments Authority
24, Tilak Marg, New Delhi - 110 001
www.nma.gov.in

in association with

Aryan Books International
Pooja Apartments, 4B, Ansari Road,
New Delhi - 110 002
Tel.: 23287589, 23255799; Fax: 91-11-23270385
E-mail: aryanbooks@gmail.com
www.aryanbooks.co.in

Designed and Printed in India at
ABI Prints & Publishing Co., New Delhi.

To the memory of late Mrs. Debala Mitra,
former Director-General of the Archaeological Survey
of India who put Ratnagiri on the map of Buddhist Studies

Preface

It is an honour to write for the National Monuments Authority (NMA) under the Ministry of Culture, which came into existence as a result of an Act of Parliament – the Ancient Monuments and Archaeological Sites and Remains AMASR (Amendment and Validation) Act, 2010 enacted in March, 2010. NMA started functioning in November 2011 and I joined the organization in September 2012.

A new initiative that the Act proposed was the regulation of a 300 metre area around the nearly 3700 centrally protected monuments. The Act entrusted NMA with overseeing the bye-laws that would regulate this development and introduced the term heritage in the making of bye-laws. In my view it is important that we make a clear distinction between heritage and archaeology and then develop strategies for bringing the two together. It is this larger agenda that the book attempts to address.

The book draws on research conducted by me, over the last several years, on the history and archaeology of Buddhism in the subcontinent, with special reference to Odisha. This research has benefitted through support from several scholars and institutions, especially the Archaeological Survey of India and the Jawaharlal Nehru University. I am also thankful to Prof. A.K. Pattanayak, Vice Chancellor, Utkal University of Culture, Prof. K.K. Basa, Department of Anthropology, Utkal University and Dr. Sunil Kumar Patnaik, Secretary, Orissan Institute of Maritime and South-east Asian Studies, Bhubaneswar for the invitation to participate in the International Conference on 'Buddhist Heritage of Odisha: Situating Odisha in the Global Perspective' held at Udayagiri from 1st to 3rd February, 2013.

Himanshu Prabha Ray

March 11, 2013 — Chairperson, NMA

Contents

List of Illustrations

Photographs courtesy: Dr. Debdutta Ray, unless otherwise stated.

Chapter 1

Introduction

CONFERENCE ON BUDDHISM AT UDAYGIRI TO PROMOTE TOURISM

This was the headline of an article in *The Times of India*, Bhubaneswar, dated January 21, 2013 announcing a three-day meeting of 120 scholars of Buddhism held at the Buddhist site of Udayagiri in Jajpur district of Odisha from 1st to 3rd of February 2013. The meeting was organized by the Odisha Culture and Tourism Department and in addition to art-historians and archaeologists, the meeting also included tour operators. Nor was this the only newspaper to report on the international conference, which was covered by both the print and electronic media in Bhubaneswar.

On this occasion, the relic excavated from another Buddhist site—that of Lalitgiri—was displayed in the Orissa State Museum acceding to a long-standing demand of the State, as was widely reported in the media under the title, 'Buddha Tooth to Find Place in Odisha Museum,' *The Times of India* (Bhubaneswar, August 19, 2012). After the conclusion of the conference, the media announced that: 'Buddhist meet clinches world heritage status cry for Udayagiri' (*The Times of India*, Bhubaneswar, February 4, 2013). This 'cry' was raised by a local institution based at Udayagiri known as the Udayagiri Ashram of the International Indecency Prevention Movement (http://www.iipmsovaniya.org accessed on 8th March 2013), a movement based on principles of introspection and self-purification.

The organization and publicity of the conference raises several issues relating to the archaeology of Buddhist sites, their protection and preservation and the link with the promotion of tourism, which is considered a major revenue-earner for the state. Is the primary purpose of protecting monuments economic and geared towards the promotion of tourism? Monuments are often described as a nation's heritage. What does the term, 'heritage', imply and how is this to be defined? The inevitable issue is: how do local communities settled in villages around the archaeological sites relate to them?

"A recent order from the Archaeological Survey of India (ASI) restricting construction activities around Buddhist monuments at Ratnagiri in Jajpur district has given rise to protests among local residents. Tourist inflow to the world-famous historical monuments has dwindled as local villagers resort to *dharna*, road blockades and other forms of protest in an attempt to make the authorities withdraw the order. Sources said, in its order communicated to Ratnagiri panchayat office, the ASI said no construction or renovation would be allowed within 100 to 300-metre radius of the world-famous Buddhist monuments at Ratnagiri. Construction or renovation can be made subject to permission from the ASI," the communiquè had said.

The order has irked around 270 house owners who have been living within this 100- to 300-metre zone for decades. "We have been residing near the monument site for ages. Our houses are located within 300 metre of the archaeological site. Suddenly, the ASI directs us not to renovate or repair our houses", said Sachidananda Mallik, Secretary, Ratnagiri Vikash Manch.

Villagers said they had asked the authorities to relocate them with suitable compensation. "We should be given an alternative site to move to. We should be given suitable compensation before relocation as we will have to lose our buildings and homestead land", said Bishnu Charan Mohanty, former zilla parishad member" (*The Telegraph*, Calcutta, January 7, 2011).

This news report adds another dimension to the discussion—how are the requirements and demands of communities living in the vicinity of monuments to be addressed? In the case of the villagers of Ratnagiri, the villagers oppose any attempts at restricting their access to the 'Buddhist' site on the grounds that this would impede their right to worship at the ancient temple of Mahakali located on the archaeological mound. Scholars, on the other hand, identify the image under worship as that of the Buddhist deity Mahakala. These competing interests need to be brought into focus, though they are not easy to resolve. Perhaps a theoretical understanding of the issues involved may not be out of place as we attempt to provide insights into the Buddhist heritage of Odisha through the archaeology of its monuments and the relevance of the past for the present and future generations.

DEFINING ARCHAEOLOGY AND HERITAGE

Archaeology and heritage are often conflated and used interchangeably. Recent scholarly literature, however, emphasizes that an unambiguous distinction needs to be made between the two (Waterton and Smith 2009). Archaeology largely deals with the material aspects of culture, as evidenced by monuments, archaeological sites and artefacts. Heritage, on the other hand, is linked to questions of identity, especially regional or local identity, memory and sense of place. Historical memory and identity, which in turn are determined largely by contemporary preferences, are considered two critical components of cultural heritage.

Historical memory can be conceived of as an intentional attempt to store and reproduce knowledge of the past. In this conceptualization, monuments and ritual become two of the potent media for the storage and recycling of historical memory (Lowenthal 1985: 210). Monuments enshrine diverse kinds of memories: memory of the vision of the builder; memory acquired over time; and finally, the created memory through transformation of the monument, either through its destruction, or by altering its context or form. Monuments also become sites for enactment of rituals, such as pilgrimage or other forms of congregation for the replenishment of memory and knowledge of the past. Social carriers of memory are the agents for the continuity of historical memory and traditionally these have included story-tellers, singers or actors who narrate mythical and past events to a local audience. The social carriers changed with the advent of modernity when the past was 'discovered' as a field of 'objective truth'. The charismatic position of the myth producers was now taken by professional 'experts'. The rise of the expert also affected the relationship between the experts and the lay audience thus resulting in the demise of 'public history'. How can historical memory be retrieved? A case in point is the Mauryan ruler (317–186 BC) Asoka, who may perhaps be described as the first royal pilgrim, as we will discuss in the next section.

HISTORICAL MEMORY AND ASOKA

The best known monuments associated with Asoka are his edicts engraved on rocks and pillars, which refer to his *dhammayata* or travel for visiting sites associated with the Buddha. Obligatory pilgrimage and rituals thus linked monuments within a larger pan Indian context and laid the foundation of an extensive religious and cultural ethos extending across the subcontinent (Ray 2012). This is an issue that we will discuss in the next chapter with reference to the two Asokan inscriptions found in Odisha. Here we will raise the question: how was the memory of King Asoka kept alive, especially since knowledge of the script in which his inscriptions were written was lost? It was only in 1837 that James Prinsep (1799-1840), the assay master of the mint at Calcutta at the time of the East India Company, was able, after much study, to decipher these ancient inscriptions.

The most famous monuments associated with Asoka elsewhere in the subcontinent are the free-standing pillars, which bear his writings. It is also evident that in many cases, large monastic establishments developed around the pillar edicts, which preserved the association of the Buddhist king Asoka with the pillars. For example, an eleventh-century pedestal inscription found at Sarnath records the restoration of the stupa of Asoka at Sarnath and its *dharmacakra* by two brothers from Gauda, identified with eastern India (Vogel 1990: 222-23). It is evident from this and other documents that Buddhist monastic complexes and texts continued to preserve the memory of what they described as the Buddhist king Asoka.

Not only did the pillar become a part of monastic architecture in the post-Asokan period, but the pillars were shifted by later kings who often also inscribed them with their own messages. Two Asokan pillars were shifted to Delhi by Firuz Shah Tughlak in AD 1367 and a description of the removal of these pillars is given in a contemporary historian's account (Page 1937). Others were re-inscribed. For example, in the fifth century AD, Samudragupta inscribed the Allahabad-Kausambi pillar of Asoka with his *prasasti* or eulogy, and the pillar also records the visit of raja Birbal, a prominent courtier of the Mughal emperor Akbar (1542–1605). Subsequently, his successor Jehangir (1569-1627) added another inscription to this pillar recording his ancestry. How is this multi-layered past to be understood?

DIVERSITY IN SOUTH ASIA

Two aspects of historical memory in South Asia are striking: one, the religious diversity; and second, the interconnectedness of diverse shrines and monuments through travel, such as pilgrimage. The diversity encompasses a wide variety of groups with distinctive ethnicity, language, religion and culture and is nowhere more marked than in the range and variety of religious architecture in South Asia from the third-second centuries BC onwards. A shrine not only functioned as a place of worship and ritual, but also as a centre for religious festivities and discourses on ethics and moral values. The rulers, merchants and others often made lavish donations and inscribed these within the precincts of the shrine. The shrine undeniably was at the core of the cultural life of a community and the focal point of a range of followers, from the lay devotee to the ritual specialist, from the patron to the architect. Poets and scribes engraved their writings in praise of the deity or the genealogy of the patron on temple walls.

The variety and religious affiliation of shrines in South Asia is extraordinary and ranges from open air tree shrines to elaborate temples, monumental stupas and colossal mosques. Similarly remarkable is the sanctity accorded to certain locations, which continued to be revered by devotees of different religions. An appropriate example of this is the site of Ellora, in the Aurangabad district of the present state of Maharashtra in India (Malandara 1993). The earliest cave excavation at Ellora began in the late sixth century and was dedicated to Shiva, followed by Buddhist and Jaina caves over the next several centuries until the tenth century AD. Although the Archaeological Survey of India has categorized the Jaina monuments into five separate cave complexes (Caves 30-34), there are in actuality 23 individual cave-temples, nearly all of them containing a shrine and rock-cut Jina image (Owen 2010).

Around 3 km from the caves at Ellora is Khuldabad, known as the valley of saints as it is said to contain the graves of 1500 Sufi saints, as well as the tomb of the Mughal Emperor Aurangzeb, those of his sons and his generals. Marking the Chisti establishment at the site are the tombs of Sayyad Burhan-al din, a Sufi saint who died in 1344, and the mausoleum of Sayyed Zain-ud-din, another saint highly revered by the Muslims. On the east side, it contains a number of verses inscribed from the *Quran* and the date of the saint's death in 1370 CE. These tombs are important markers of the fourteenth century Sufi tradition of Nizamuddin Auliya that went from Delhi to the Deccan and established itself in Khuldabad (Suvorova 2004). Ellora is not the only example of religious pluralism in South Asia, but is instead one of the many sacred places that preserve diverse historical memories.

In the context of Odisha, the pattern of a multi-religious landscape is similarly striking. The present city of Bhubaneswar and its encircling hills provide evidence for the presence of Buddhism, Jainism as well as Hinduism, though their relative concentration varied over time. In the following chapters, we will focus on Buddhist architecture, but provide a brief overview of religious diversity here (Figure 1.1).

The Udayagiri and Khandagiri hills located 6 km west of Bhubaneswar with 18 and 15 rock-cut caves respectively, provide early evidence of the presence of Jainism in Odisha. The hills are referred to as Kumari-parvata in the 17-line inscription of King Kharavela of the Mahameghavahana dynasty

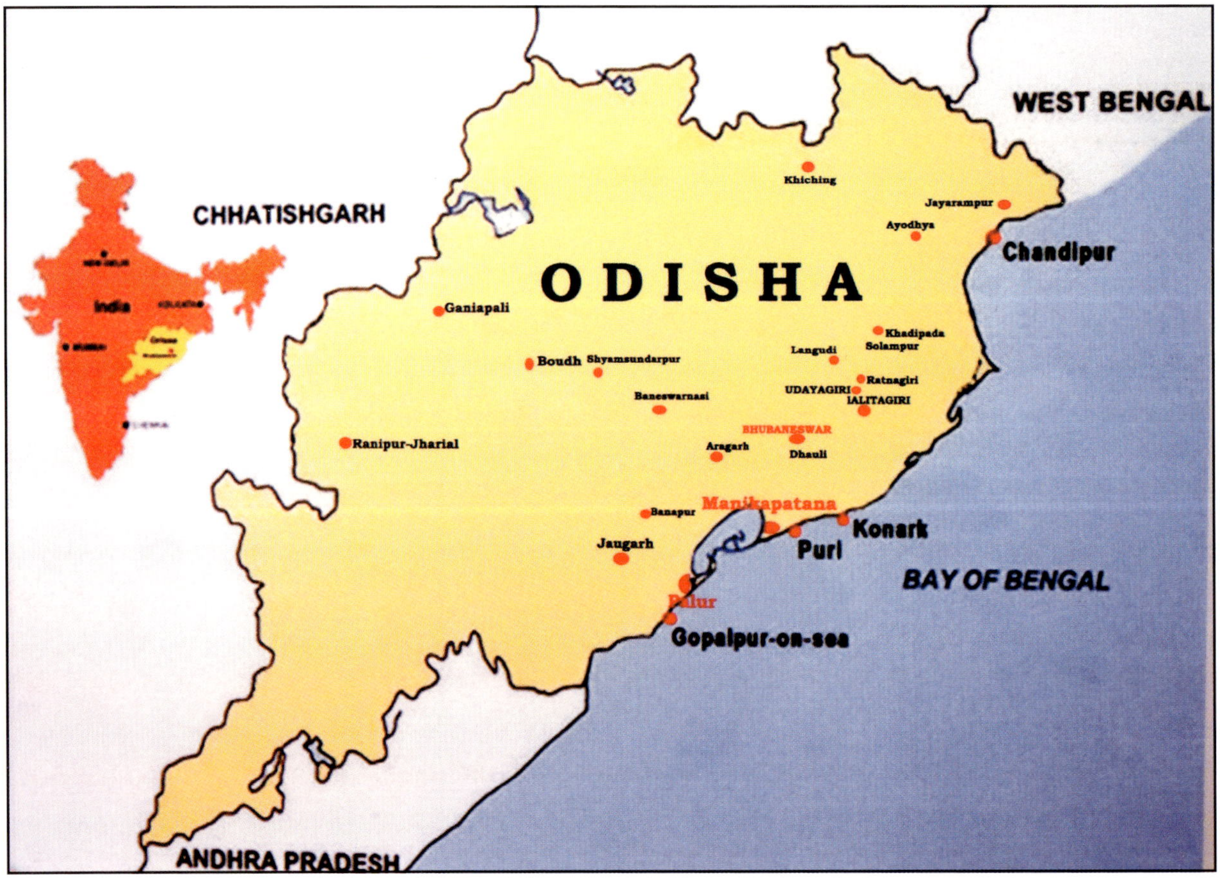

Fig. 1.1. Map showing major archaeological sites in Odisha.

Fig. 1.2. Tenth century Muktesvara temple dedicated to Siva at Bhubaneswar. The Odisha State Tourism regularly organizes a dance festival in the temple, which was held this year from 14th to 16th January 2013.

dated to the first century BC and engraved on the brow of the rock over cave 14, also known as Hathigumpha, or elephant cave. The inscription was first noticed by A. Stirling in 1820 who published an eye copy of it in *Asiatick Researches,* XV. The caves, termed *lenas* in the inscriptions, were dwelling retreats or dormitories for Jaina ascetics and opened out directly into a verandah or open space in front. An apsidal structure made of laterite blocks was found on the summit of the hill.

Line 17 of Kharavela's inscription refers to the king as having repaired several *devayatana*'s or houses of god. This is perhaps the earliest reference to a temple or shrine in Odisha, though its structural manifestation or religious affiliation is far from clear. A three-line Prakrit inscription of Maharaja Gana of third century AD found on a stone lintel near Bhadrak issued in the 8th regnal year of the king states that a person named Mulajapa installed three images in a *devayatana*. These images of Brahma, Vishnu and Maheshwar are indicative of the religious landscape of early Odisha where all three major Hindu deities

Fig. 1.3. The exquisitely carved chlorite door-frame with Gaja-Lakshmi on the façade of the monastery at Ratnagiri marks the high water-mark of decorative art of Odisha.

were revered and worshipped. At least eight inscriptions are known prior to the sixth century AD, which refer to donations to temples and though architectural fragments are found, there is almost a complete absence of structural remains from this early period.

From the sixth century AD onwards, there was an expansion of Buddhist monastic sites across Odisha, as will be discussed in Chapter 3. This period also saw the emergence of the Kalinga style of Hindu temple in its fully developed form (Figure 1.2), reaching its culmination in the eleventh century Lingaraja temple dedicated to Harihara, a combined form of Vishnu and Shiva. Under active worship, the shrine comprises a sanctum, a closed hall, a dancing hall and a hall of offerings. It thus reflects and epitomizes a complex ritual that developed during the medieval period. Legend has it that an underground

Fig. 1.4. Seated Buddha on the façade of the brick shrine at Udayagiri.

river originating under the Lingaraja temple fills the nearby Bindusagar tank. The water of the tank is known for its healing qualities and a bath in it is considered sacred.

A thirteenth century Sanskrit treatise—the *Ekamra Purana*—indicates that the deity of Lingaraja temple was originally under a mango (*ekamra*) tree and was not seen as *lingam* in earlier *yugas*, but was only revealed in the present Kali age. The name *ekamra* is mentioned in the Anantavasudeva inscription of Paramarddi (AD 1200-1278), which praises "the province of Utkala where lies the holy place of Ekamra ..... adorned with hundreds of mango-groves, wherein exists a single Devakula (temple) surrounded by numerous temples". This epigraph describes "the holy place (*ksetra*) of Ekamra as very dear to god Krittivasa, well known for bestowing divine achievements and always decorated with flowers of every season" (Panigrahi, 1981: 219). The Brahmesvara inscription of Udyotakesari Mahabhavagupta IV also describes Ekamra as Siddhaksetra.

There are significant reciprocal influences between the Hindu and Buddhist art and architecture of Odisha, such as in door frame fragments from Ratnagiri, Udayagiri and Lalitgiri. While the image on the lintel at Ratnagiri is that of Gajalaksmi (Figure 1.3), at Udayagiri (Figure 1.4) it is a seated Buddha flanked by Avalokitesvara and Vajrapani (Donaldson 2001: 376-77).

One of the issues that the survey of religious architecture presented here raises is the extent to which Buddhist monasteries were a reflection of the practice of the religion within a regional cultural milieu. The image of Mahakala, which was being worshipped at Ratnagiri (Figure 1.5) at the time of its excavations in 1958 as the Hindu goddess Mahakali, is itself an adaptation of a Hindu deity into Buddhism. A six-armed form of the god from Ratnagiri is now in the Patna museum (Donaldson, 2001: 230-32). Was this only a case of shared artistic traditions between the two religious communities in eastern India? Did this similarity extend to all monastic sites or are inter-site differences significant? A comparison of the plans of the monastic complexes at Ratnagiri, Udayagiri and Lalitgiri provides evidence of inter-site variations.

Facing Page:
Fig. 1.5. The renovated Mahakala temple at Ratnagiri. It was earlier on the mound and enshrined a two-armed image of the deity worshipped by the villagers as Mahakali.

Different forms of prayer and worship marked the spread of Islam in the subcontinent. The emphasis in Islam was on congregational prayer, which required a large courtyard with a prayer-hall at the western end. The western side was occupied by an alcove or recess termed the *mihrab* and indicated the direction of prayer to be offered. In addition, a distinct form of burial in a tomb was practiced, especially in the case of the elite. From 1568 to 1751, Cuttack was the headquarters of Mughal rule in the region. It is here that mosques, tombs, palaces and forts of the Mughal period survive (Yamin 2009). The challenge is to blend this multi-layered history of religious architecture in the Bhubaneswar-Cuttack region with modernity and urban planning. Laws promulgated for the regulation of areas around the monuments need to be in harmony with the diverse religious landscape and help protect and maintain the plural cultural fabric within the larger pan-Indian context.

MOBILITY AND TRAVEL IN BUDDHISM

Buddha *dhamma* was one of the ascetic movements that rose in the middle of the first millennium BC. It distinguished itself from Upanishadic thought and Jain tenets by redefining karma and liberation. The eightfold path shown by the Buddha was founded on wisdom, morality and concentration (Berkwitz 2010: 10). Like other contemporary Indic religions, Buddha *dhamma* had no central organization, "no single authoritative text, no simple set of defining practices" (Kinnard, 2011: ix). Its core principle was refuge in the Buddha, the *Dhamma* and the Sangha, though as it expanded across Asia it absorbed local traditions, responded to historical factors and evolved philosophically.

The physical manifestations of the *dhamma* appeared in the archaeological record at least two to three hundred years later in the form of inscriptions, stupas, images and other objects of veneration. Relic and image worship were important features in the expansion of Buddhism across the subcontinent and into other parts of Asia. The issue that is addressed here relates to the agency responsible for the spread of Buddhism across the Indian subcontinent and the setting up of monastic establishments. Was it the ruler and the state, as indicated by Asokan inscriptions, or was it the Buddhist monks and nuns, as evident from records of donations and gifts to religious sites (Ray 1986: 104-07)?

In contrast to Sanchi in Central India, where 200 of the 631 inscriptions record donations by monks and nuns, at Kanheri, near the present city of Mumbai on the west coast, the single largest group of donors (as mentioned in 19 inscriptions) comprises *negamas* (merchants), *vanija* (trader), *suvanakokara* (goldsmith) and *heranika* (treasurer). The Buddhist texts, at the same time, credit merchants and trading groups with the setting up of religious shrines, as for example in the case of merchant Anathapindaka's purchase of the park known as the Jetavana in order to present it to the Buddha and his monks for their use as a monastic establishment. This is a theme that finds representation at several early Buddhist sites, such as Bharhut, Bodh Gaya, Sannathi, Amaravati, etc. How valid are these statements in the context of Odisha where both early donator inscriptions and narrative sculptures are rare? When was Buddhism established in the region and how?

A third century AD Prakrit inscription from Nagarjunakonda in Andhra refers to the fraternities of monks at Tosali, Palur and Puspagiri, identified as major Buddhist centres in Odisha (*Epigraphia Indica* XX: 23). Recent archaeological research has brought to light 120 Buddhist sites in Odisha. Of these, only eight are centrally protected, while a majority remain unprotected. As will be discussed in Chapter 3, several sites have earlier beginnings, one of these being Langudi, on a low hill running from north to south, located in the plains of the Mahanadi Delta about 90 km from Bhubaneswar in the Jajpur district, though most of the sculptures date from seventh to ninth century AD. Archaeological excavations at Lalitgiri have provided evidence for a second-first century BC stupa, an apsidal shrine built over the remains of an earlier structure, inscriptions in Kushana-Brahmi, Gupta and post-Gupta script, as also a Gupta coin. Relics in gold foil were found at the site and will be discussed in detail in Chapter 4 (Bandyopadhyay 2007: 9-10).

In the context of eastern India, the *Vinaya* (Mahavagga, First Khanndaka, 4) records that two early disciples of the Buddha, the merchants Tapussa and Bhallika travelled from Ukkala, often identified with Odisha, to where the Buddha was meditating under the Bodhi tree and presented him with rice cakes and honey. They are also credited with establishing caityas and monastic complexes on their return. This story no doubt links important merchants with patronage to Buddhism and to the setting up of stupas. More importantly, it provides insights into the world of travel and trade and its close connection with monks. Was travel restricted to overland routes or is there evidence for coastal Odisha's involvement in maritime systems?

BUDDHISM AND THE EAST COAST MARITIME NETWORK

An issue that requires consideration at this stage relates to the extent and vigour of the trading network linking eastern India with the Bay of Bengal and evidence for the spread of Buddhism across the ocean. A cluster of fifth century inscriptions of unambiguous Buddhist affiliation was found in Kedah on the west coast of the Malay Peninsula. Three of these inscriptions were made of local stone and bear similar illustrations of Buddhist stupas. Texts very similar to these inscriptions have been found on the island of Borneo and on the coast of Brunei (Christie 1995: 256). The most interesting of these inscriptions in Sanskrit is that of Buddhagupta, which refers to the setting up of the stone by the mariner Buddhagupta, resident of Raktamrittika, identified with Rajbadidanga in Bengal, on the successful completion of his voyage (Figure 1.6 and 1.7; Chhabra 1965: 23-24).

Fig. 1.6. Stone inscription of about the seventh century AD now in Indian Museum Kolkata which refers to the setting up of the stone by the mariner Buddhagupta, resident of Raktamrttika, often identified with Rajbadidanga in Bengal, on the successful completion of his voyage.

The *Ye dhamma....* verse has perhaps the most extensive circulation in the Buddhist world and occurs on stone images, clay tablets, metal plaques and on palm-leaf, paper and cloth. The stanza was spoken not by the Buddha, but by Assaji, one of the group of five monks converted to Buddhism at Sarnath. This event is narrated only once in the Vinayas of the various schools, and the verse occurs once only in the *Tripitakas*. Yet, its popularity across South and Southeast Asia is truly remarkable.

Fig. 1.7. Buddhagupta inscription (side view).

The full stanza reads:

ye dhamma hetuppabhava yesam hetum tathagato aha
tesan ca yo nirodho evamvadi mahasamano ti.

(The Tathagata has declared the cause and also the cessation
Of the things (dhamma) that arise from causes:
Such is the teaching of the Great Samana) (Skilling 2003-4: 273-87).

In the earliest Indian examples, the verse was inscribed on stupas and by the middle of the first millennium AD, stone images frequently carried it. This practice is not widely known in Southeast Asia, though there are examples of inscribed stone Buddha images from central Thailand (Figure 1.8 and 1.9).

In addition are moulded images of Buddhas, Bodhisattvas, stupas and so on that are ubiquitous at North Indian Buddhist sites from the sixth century onwards and are found extensively in Southeast Asia. Based on descriptions provided by Xuanzang, it is evident that the production of sealings was linked to merit-making and cleansing of sin. To produce an image of the Buddha or to produce a stupa brought merit. Miniature stupas and images were produced in large numbers and were ritually placed inside relic chambers of stupas, which were then sealed. Xuanzang wrote about Jayasena who lived in Rajagriha (present Rajgir) in the seventh century:

It is a custom in India to make little stupas of powdered scent made into a paste; their height is about six or seven inches, and they place inside them some written extract from a *sutra*; this they call a *dharmasarira* (fa-shi-li). When the number of these become large, they then build a great stupa, and collect all the others within it, and continually offer to it religious offerings (Beal, 1981: 146-47).

There was a shift in maritime networks around the middle of the first millennium AD and pilgrims visiting sites associated with the life of the Buddha formed a major category of travellers. The Chinese pilgrim Faxian arrived overland in India in AD 399 and returned by sea to China in AD 413–14 from Sri Lanka heading towards the northwest tip of Sumatra. The ship was wrecked on the way and perhaps landed in the Andamans. The next phase took Faxian to the northwest of Borneo where he arrived in 414 after 90 days at sea. The pilgrim remained in Borneo for five months and then left for China in mid-414 heading towards Canton. The ninth century marked a turning point and several major coastal sites in peninsular Malaysia date to this period, such as Ko Kho Kao near Takuapa, Laem Pho near Chaiya in Thailand and Kampong Sungai Mas in south Kedah in Malaysia known for large collections of Chinese as well as West Asia ceramics. Other characteristic features of these sites are the brick architectural remains that survive and have been unearthed in archaeological excavations, as well as stone statuary, both Hindu and Buddhist (Jacq-Hergoualc'h, 2002: 134-60).

Fig. 1.8. Image of the Pala-Sena period showing seated Buddha in the centre surrounded by scenes from his life and found at Ratchaburana temple, Ayyuthaya, Thailand.

The most interesting information about circum-peninsular navigation is contained in Yijing's accounts of the voyage of the Chinese pilgrims who travelled to India and returned during the second half of the seventh century AD. Of the sixty monks whose trip is briefly recounted, at least thirty-seven travelled by sea on merchant ships and none seemed to have been aware of the possibility of crossing the isthmus of Kra, even if some of them stopped off there, notably in Langkasuka. Yijing also provides an account of his own journey from Canton in October-November with the northeast monsoon and reached Palembang a month later. He stayed there for six months, then went to Jambi near Palembang sometime around May. He stayed there for two months and then re-embarked in order to take advantage of the winds of the southwest monsoon to reach Kedah (Jiecha). He did not leave this region for India until the beginning of the following year when the northeast monsoon was well established. He reached the Nicobar islands in ten days and fifteen days later arrived at Tamralipti in Bengal. This was clearly the most convenient route to the holy places of historic Buddhism (Jacq-Hergoualc'h, 2002: 53).

Fig. 1.9. 'Ye *dhamma*...' verse on the back of the image. The verse articulates several layers of meanings: it captures the Enlightenment experience of the Buddha at Bodh Gaya; links this essence to the *dhamma* or the true body of the Buddha, thereby introducing fluidity between the abstract and the physical; historically this critical text was enshrined in stupas across Asia, as a measure that would result in rejuvenating the Sangha and help the lay community renew its vows to the Buddha.

The active role of the Buddhist clergy in the propagation of certain texts is also being increasingly emphasised. For example, the *Gandavyuha* enjoyed great prestige and popularity among the Buddhist communities of Indonesia, China and Japan. The Chinese obtained the text from Khotan and propagated it in at least three different versions all over the Far East. In the third and last translation, the *Gandavyuha* occurs as an individual text and not as a part of the larger collection of the *Avatamsakasutra*. The preservation and propagation of the *Gandavyuha* text in Indonesia may perhaps be discussed from a different perspective, i.e., its study and dissemination in the monastic establishments. More importantly, its prominent sculptural representation at Borobudur in central Java highlights the significance of religious travel in early Javanese society.

It is then evident that in addition to trade and trading networks, pilgrimage and religious travel provided an impetus for mobility across South Asia as well as across the Bay of Bengal into Southeast Asia and China. It is also accepted that worship of the relics played a key role in the spread of Buddhism across Asia and relics have served to forge a distinctive Buddhist geography articulated through pilgrimage routes. Three types of relics are indicated in early Buddhist tradition, viz., corporeal relics (bones, teeth, hair, nail-clippings, etc. of the Buddha), relics of use (Buddha's staff, robe, begging bowl), and relics of commemoration (images, copper-plates with the Buddhist creed). The relics were "thought to retain—to be infused with, impregnated with—the qualities that animated and defined the living Buddha" (Schopen 1997: 160). This is an issue that we will discuss in Chapter 4.

DID BUDDHISM DECLINE?

Scholars have stressed that the interaction between Buddha *dhamma* and Hinduism was a two-way process, with reformulation of ideas from the former into the latter. One of the forms of Tara, called the Mahacinakrama Tara, was adopted from an eleventh century Buddhist Tantric *sadhana* into the thirteenth century Hindu *Phetkarinitantra* as Ugra Tara, a popular goddess in North India.

There is another hypothesis that in Odisha the religion did not disappear but went underground and survived in the form of a 'crypto-Buddhism' (a combination of Tantric, Buddhist, and Vaisnava elements), its echoes surfacing several centuries later in the Mahima Dharma movement of the nineteenth century (Basu 1982). Founded by Mahima Gosavi, this movement combined social protest with *bhakti* and had certain Buddhist elements in its ideas and organization (Omveldt 2003: 225-27).

The relationship between the different religious traditions of the subcontinent was complex and no simple answers are possible. In Odishan sculpture, from tenth century onwards, the Buddha is depicted seated in *dhyana-mudra* in *dasavatara* sets on the back slab of Vishnu images. The Buddha *avatar* wears the robes of a monk and has elongated ears. With the emergence of the Jagannatha cult in the thirteenth century, Buddha is often identified with Jagannatha. In late *dasavatara* panels, either Buddha or Jagannatha may appear as the ninth *avatar* of Vishnu. An inscription on the Somesvara temple at Ranipur Jharial in Orissa refers to the Buddha as one of the four deities enshrined in the temple, the others being the Siva-linga, Karttikeya and Gaja-Lakshmi (Donaldson, 2001: 409-414).

The Buddha as an avatar of Vishnu was further popularized in Odisha by the Sanskrit poet Jayadeva who lived around AD 1200. Several legends relating to Jayadeva associate him with the Jagannatha temple at Puri, which was built under the patronage of the Ganga kings of coastal Orissa. His famous *dasavatara stotra* recounted the ten *avatars* of the deity including that of the Buddha. By linking Buddha's condemnation of Vedic ritual with his compassion for the animal victims, Jayadeva provided a positive perspective to the inclusion of Sakyamuni. This *stotra* or verse became very popular and was recited and sung along with Jayadeva's other epic creation, the *Gita Govinda*. The *Gita Govinda* was composed specifically for dance performances for Lord Jagannatha worshipped as the supreme form of Vishnu in the temple at Puri. It initiated a trend for the inclusion of dance and music in temple veneration.

Jayadeva's composition quickly found a pan-Indian audience. A stone inscription of Maharaja Sarangadeva Vaghela (13th century Gujarat) opens with Jayadeva's invocation of the ten forms of Krishna. An Oriya language inscription on the left side of the Jaya-Vijaya doorway of the Jagannath temple dated AD 1499 prescribes the performance of the *Gita Govinda*. Dancing was to be performed before the deities at the time of *bhoga* or food offerings and was to continue from the time of their evening meal to their bedtime meal (Miller, 1977: 6). Thus, the relations between Buddhism and Hinduism were once again configured to reflect ground realities. How do monuments echo these changing relations? We do know that the categorization and protection of monuments was the result of transformations in the law at the beginning of the twentieth century. How has the experience of the last century helped evolve better conservation practices? Are these adequate to preserve monuments against challenges of development and modernity? These are issues that will be addressed in the final chapter. The objective of the book will be to aid in the integration of the needs of archaeology and heritage in Odisha with tourism and future urban planning.

Chapter 2

Asoka's Message of Compassion

When he had been consecrated eight years, the Beloved of the Gods, the king Piyadassi [Asoka] conquered Kalinga [identified with parts of modern Odisha]. A hundred and fifty thousand people were deported, a hundred thousand were killed and many times that number perished. Afterwards, now that Kalinga was annexed, the Beloved of the Gods very earnestly practised *Dhamma*, desired *Dhamma* and taught *Dhamma*.

On conquering Kalinga the Beloved of the Gods felt remorse, for, when an independent country is conquered the slaughter, death and deportation of the people is extremely grievous to the Beloved of the Gods, and weighs heavily on his mind. What is even more deplorable to the Beloved of the Gods, is that those who dwelt there, whether brahmanas or sramanas or those of other sects, or householders who show obedience to their superiors, obedience to mother and father, obedience to their teachers and behave well and devotedly towards their friends, acquaintances, colleagues, relatives, slaves, and servants– all suffer violence, murder, and separation from their loved ones (XIII Major Rock Edict of the Mauryan king Asoka, who ruled from 274/3 to 232/1 BC, inscribed at Girnar in Gujarat. Thapar 1998: 255-56).

The Major Rock Edicts, consisting of a set of fourteen proclamations inscribed on rocks, occur across the Indian subcontinent from Shahbazgarhi in Peshawar district of modern Pakistan to sites in

Fig. 2.1. Rock Edict of Asoka engraved on the hill of Dhauli near Bhubaneswar.

Andhra Pradesh in South India. Rock Edict XIII is the largest in the group and it is here that Asoka expresses remorse at the loss of life in the war in Kalinga. It would seem that the term Kalinga denoted an area that extended from the Cuttack-Puri region to present Ganjam-Srikakulam districts. It should be remembered that the term Kalinga had varying connotations at different periods of history and at times extended as far as the Godavari-Krishna delta on the Andhra coast (Brandtner, 2001: 179-201). Rock Edict XIII, however, is not to be found within the present state of Odisha and is replaced by the two separate edicts both at Jaugada on the north bank of the Rishikulya River in Ganjam district and at Dhauli on the banks of the river Daya, 8 km south of Bhubaneswar (Figure 2.1).

Facing Page:
Fig. 2.2. Map showing distribution of edicts of Asoka in the subcontinent.

The Dhauli and Jaugada edicts are addressed to the officials at Tosali and Samapa respectively indicating the names of ancient settlements near the two sites. The Separate Edicts exhort the officers to gain the affection and confidence of the people whom Asoka regarded as his children and to promote *dhamma*

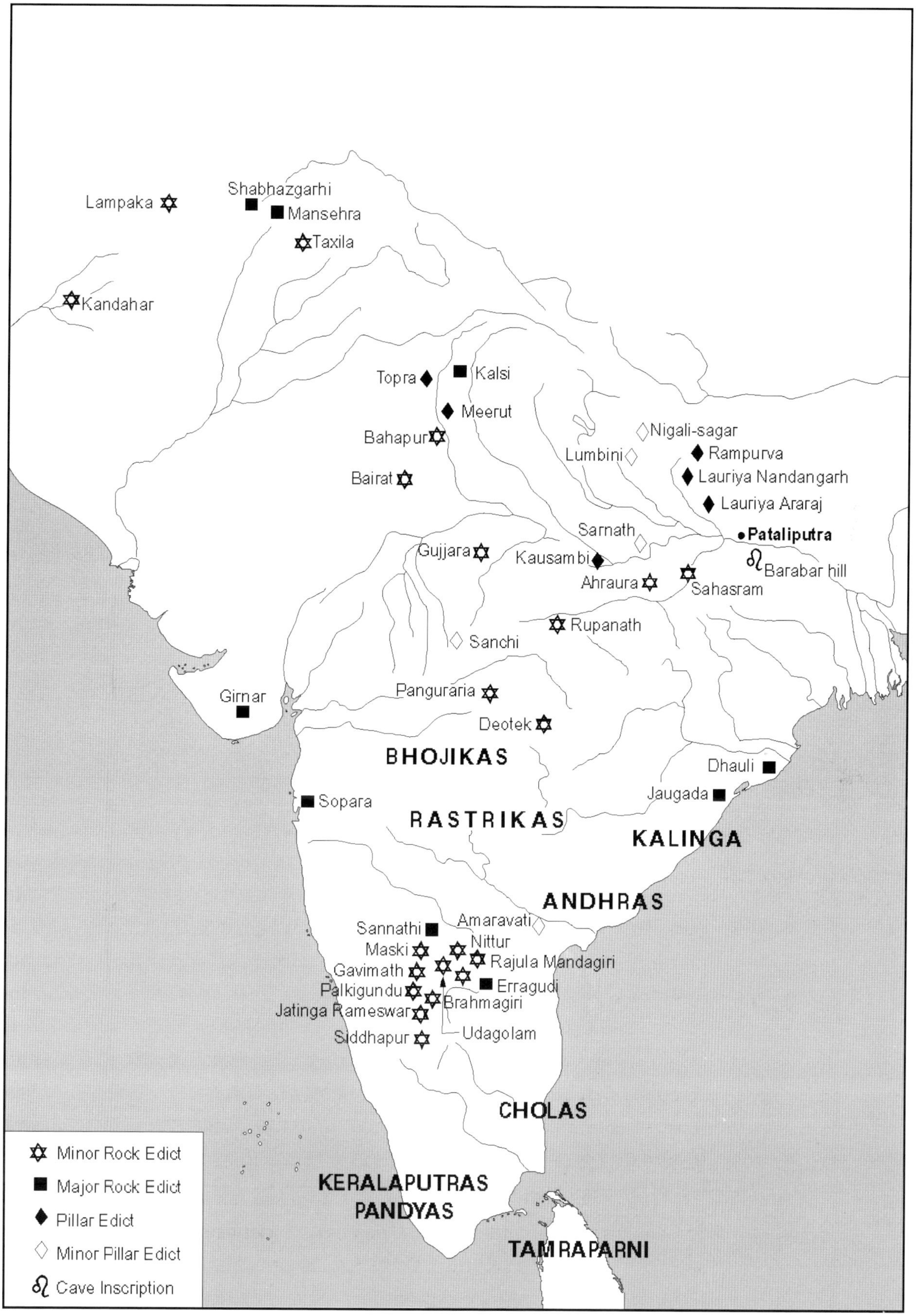

Lampaka
Shabhazgarhi
Mansehra
Taxila
Kandahar
Topra
Kalsi
Meerut
Bahapur
Bairat
Nigali-sagar
Lumbini
Rampurva
Lauriya Nandangarh
Lauriya Araraj
Sarnath
Pataliputra
Gujjara
Kausambi
Barabar hill
Ahraura
Sahasram
Rupanath
Sanchi
Girnar
Panguraria
Deotek
BHOJIKAS
Dhauli
Jaugada
Sopara
RASTRIKAS
KALINGA
ANDHRAS
Sannathi
Amaravati
Maski
Nittur
Gavimath
Rajula Mandagiri
Palkigundu
Erragudi
Brahmagiri
Jatinga Rameswar
Udagolam
Siddhapur
CHOLAS
KERALAPUTRAS
PANDYAS
TAMRAPARNI
Minor Rock Edict
Major Rock Edict
Pillar Edict
Minor Pillar Edict
Cave Inscription

Fig. 2.3. On the north face of Dhauli hill is the famous elephant cut out of the rock, beneath which are engraved Asoka's edicts.

among them. The edicts were to be proclaimed every four months on the eighth day of the appearance of the auspicious star Tisya and were to be read aloud to the people, as also at regular intervals in-between. Clearly, Asoka's message of compassion and empathy for the people was emphasized in the two Separate Edicts in Odisha, but very differently from that which was decreed in other parts of the subcontinent. Scholars are increasingly of the view that there were linguistic variations in Asoka's epigraphs, as well as differences in nature and content and that these changes were based on local and regional contexts. Besides, ritualized public recitations of the inscriptions would also have been adapted to suit local contexts (Olivelle 2012: 158-59). The prevailing conditions in the eastern parts of the empire required different strategies to be adopted, as compared to other parts of the subcontinent. Nevertheless, Kalinga was by no means an isolated space and the next section places these within a pan-Indian context (Figure 2.2).

THE EDICTS IN A PAN-INDIAN CONTEXT

Asoka's grandfather Chandragupta had founded the Mauryan dynasty and established its rule in large parts of the Ganga Valley and the north-west, but it was Asoka who established his supremacy over the subcontinent, as evident from his edicts. In Major Rock Edict II, Asoka refers to the people on the frontiers—the Greek ruler Antiochus in the north-west and the Ceras, Colas, Pandyas, etc. in the far south. Rock Edict V alludes to officers responsible for the establishment and promotion of *dhamma* (or dharma) even among the Greeks (yavanas), Kambojas and others resident on the western borders of his dominions, while Rock Edict XIII refers to his victories over the Greek king yavanaraja Antiyoka and others bordering his dominions, such as Ptolemy, Antigonus, Magas and Alexander.

Asokan inscriptions are unique in the history of India in many ways. These inscriptions may be classified into Rock Edicts (Major and Minor), cave inscriptions, and Pillar Edicts. The Minor Rock Edicts are also said to form the earliest group of Asokan inscriptions, followed by the Major Rock Edicts. The Pillar Edicts were the last to be promulgated. Their distribution is largely restricted to the Ganga Valley and no example of these has so far been found in Odisha or in peninsular India (Salomon 1998: 136). The inscriptions were engraved on free-standing rocks and

Fig. 2.4. Rock-cut monolithic elephant and pillars at the base of Kaima hillock in Jajpur district.

pillars, instead of within religious establishments. They also differ in their tone, form and content from later inscriptions, which either record donations or grants of land or else detailed genealogies and achievements of the rulers. The later inscriptions seldom present a king's vision of *dhamma* for his people, as the Asokan inscriptions do. Asoka's epigraphs contain his exhortations in stone, rather than records of the king's glory.

Scholars refer to two genres of Asokan inscriptions: those in the first person and those that refer to the king in the third person. While in almost all the Pillar Edicts, the Separate Edicts and some of the Major Rock Edicts, the king speaks in the first person directly to his officials and to specific groups of people, the others refer to him in the third person and articulate his ideals of *dhamma*. Asoka used the term *dhamma-lipi* or religious writings for his edicts and expresses imperial ideology through his proclamations. Recent research has also shown that the edicts were edited and translated to suit local requirements and this is very evident in the context of Odisha. As mentioned above, in Odisha the edicts were to be read aloud on specific days. This public reading of the inscriptions shows that there would have been oral commentaries by the local officials and that copies may perhaps have been made on perishable materials, which are now lost (Olivelle 2012).

Another significant feature is the association of Asokan edicts in Odisha with the elephant, as evident from the rock-cut elephant at Dhauli above the inscribed stone (Figure 2.3). Other examples of this are known, for example at Kaima in Jajpur district. Kaima is a small hill on the banks of the river Kimira about one kilometre from its confluence with the river Brahmani and is located to the north of Langudi hill. A rock-cut elephant is known from the site located within what was perhaps an enclosure, but the only remnants now are four khondalite pillars (Figure 2.4). Did these edicts go into oblivion in the post-Mauryan period? We do know that activity continued on Dhauli hill. Archaeological excavations at the foot of the hill unearthed a temple and a well ascribable to 7th century AD (*Indian Archaeology—A Review 1962-63*: 17), while another 12th century temple of Shiva known as Dhavalesvara stands on top of the hill. In contrast, the edicts at Jaugada were enclosed within a mud fort, but its history is far from clear. An issue that scholars have long debated relates to the nature of Asoka's *dhamma*. Can this be equated to Buddha *dhamma*?

ASOKA AND HIS *DHAMMA*

In his Minor Rock Edicts, Asoka refers to himself as a Buddhist *upasaka* or lay devotee and expresses his desire that Buddhism percolate down to the lowest level to include elephant-trainers, charioteers, teachers and scribes (Sircar 1979: 12). It would seem that the southern versions all belong to a single recension, which was issued for engraving extensively on the hills at one specific time, as indicated by the reference to 256 nights. The *dhamma* of these records is largely ethical, with the injunction to: "Obey mother and father, obey the teachers; have mercy on living beings; speak the truth and propagate the *dhamma*."

The involvement of Asoka with the *dhamma* was by no means limited to propagation of an ethical way of life as is evident from his records. Asoka praises ceremonies performed for religious purposes, but decries those performed on the occasion of births, illnesses, and weddings (Rock Edict IX). There are references to several religious ceremonies in his inscriptions, such as visits to the Bodhi tree and chanting of Buddhist scriptures, among others. Rock Edict VIII dates Asoka's *dhammayata* (pilgrimage) to Sambodhi or the sacred Bodhi tree at Gaya ten years after his consecration. In the Bairat rock edict near Jaipur, Rajasthan, Asoka recommends the study and reflection of seven texts of the Buddhist canon. Minor pillar inscriptions at Allahabad, Sarnath and Sanchi (Minor Pillar Edict III) are generally referred to as schism edicts and warn monks and nuns against creating division in the Sangha. At Bodh Gaya, the installation of a polished sandstone throne (*vajrasana*) found by Cunningham in a shrine at the foot of the Bodhi tree is attributed to Asoka (*Annual Report, Archaeological Survey of India, 1908-9*: 153-54).

In spite of this active interest in the Buddhist Sangha and its affairs, the edicts of Asoka make it amply clear that the protection and support of the ruler extended beyond the Sangha to the brahmanas, all other religious mendicants, as also to all religious sects. Asoka placed Buddhism alongside Brahmanism, Jainism and the Ajivikas in his edicts and stressed that his *dhamma* was not the doctrine of one religion but was of universal acceptability (Yamazaki 1999: 17-36).

Schopen (1997: 116) suggests a close correspondence between Asokan inscriptions and the *Mahaparinibbana sutta* in which the Buddha states:

'After I have passed away, monks, those making the pilgrimage to the shrines, honouring the shrines, will come [to these places], they will speak in this way: Here the Blessed One attained the highest most excellent awakening, etc.'

In the past, scholars have constantly tried to reconcile information contained in the edicts with those from other sources, such as the biography of Asoka in Buddhist texts, like the *Asokavadana* written five hundred years after Mauryan rule in second century AD in Sanskrit. In the *Asokavadana* compiled in north-western India, Asoka is described as an unsightly prince who quelled the revolt in Taxila and ascended the throne after killing his ninety-nine brothers. His fierce and malevolent nature was tamed by the Buddhist monk, Upagupta, who is said to have converted him and inspired him to visit places associated with the life of the Buddha. According to the legend, Asoka then went on to build eighty-four thousand stupas throughout his empire. The text also includes the tragic story of his son, Kunal, who was blinded by a jealous stepmother who wanted her son to succeed to the throne.

A second text that popularized the story of Asoka was the Ceylonese chronicle, the *Mahavamsa,* dated to the late fourth or early fifth century AD. Its authorship is attributed to a Buddhist monk Mahanama who wrote under the patronage of a Sri Lankan king. In the Sri Lankan chronicles, the emphasis is on the purification of the Sangha by Asoka and the dispatch of Buddhist missionaries not only to different parts of the subcontinent, but also to Suvarnabhumi, and most of all to Sri Lanka. There are references to the Sri Lankan king Devanampiyatissa (250–210 BC) being re-consecrated by the envoys of Asoka. The text does not mention Asoka's repugnant attributes, such as his ugliness or his violent nature.

There are other major variations as well. In the *Asokavadana*, Asoka is said to have been born one hundred years after the passing away of the Buddha, while in the *Mahavamsa*, the Mauryan king was consecrated 218 years after the Buddha's *nirvana*. The *Mahavamsa* associates Asoka with holding the third Buddhist Council at Pataliputra and of cleansing the Sangha of false beliefs by the defrocking of at least sixty thousand monks. Another tradition that is mentioned in the *Mahavamsa*, but scarcely occurs in the *Asokavadana,* relates to the despatch of missionaries by Asoka to different regions.

One of the terms that Asoka used almost a hundred times in his inscriptions is *dhamma*, or dharma, and perhaps for the first time *dhamma* became a key concept in political theology. A comparison of the Asokan edicts with contemporary descriptions of kingship as enshrined in the *Dharmasastras* and the *Arthasastra* make it obvious that the *dhamma* of the edicts was not doctrinal and did not adhere to any one religion, but denoted universal law and righteousness.

Asoka insisted that his *dhamma* was based on ancient tradition, which had been ignored by past kings who governed unjustly. He termed his *dhamma* 'ancient custom' and proclaimed the revival of tradition. This is not the place to discuss the etymology of *dhamma/dharma* or changes in its meaning over time from its earliest occurrence in Vedic literature. What is undeniable is the contribution of Asoka in providing it centrality within political thinking. From the Mauryan period onwards, the righteous king became a role model for rulers to emulate. As evident from the frequent use of the term in his edicts, Asoka redefined it to make it almost entirely an ethical concept. There is no doubt that scholars will continue to debate many of these issues, and the history of Asoka will continue to enrich and impact our understanding of the present. This is an issue that we will discuss in the last section. Here, we will focus on the local archaeological context of Asoka's inscriptions; the status of Buddha *dhamma* in the post-Asokan period in Odisha; and the extent to which Buddhism took root and expanded in the region.

BUDDHISM IN THE POST-MAURYAN PERIOD

In contrast to the scattered remains of the Mauryan period, large inter-connected monastic complexes emerged elsewhere in India in the post-Asokan period. This is still an under-researched theme in the context of Odisha, though there is evidence for the expansion of sites in the period. Archaeological remnants indicate that the present city of Bhubaneswar formed an early core of the settlement. Besides coastal Odisha, there was a spatial spread into the interior parts of the state, such as at Asurgarh and Budhigarh in Kalahandi district, Nehena in Nuapada district, Manmunda in Khondmals, Sitabhinji in Keonjhar, and Biratgarh and Khijjinga in Mayurbhanja district (Yule 2006).

On the south-eastern part of Bhubaneswar about 5 kilometres from Dhauli, several seasons of archaeological excavations were conducted at the fortified

Fig. 2.5. *Sivalinga* in the twelfth century Bhaskaresvara temple at Bhubaneswar.

site of Sisupalgarh, roughly one square kilometre on plan, in 1948 and 1949 by B.B. Lal of the Archaeological Survey of India. A striking feature of the Sisupalgarh fort, quadrangular on plan, is the alignment of thirteen monolithic laterite columns that still survive and a large gateway made of dressed laterite blocks. The fort was circumscribed by the stream named Gangua or Gandhavati, which flows around Sisupalgarh. In an earlier period, the stream may have fed and drained the moat. Excavations date the occupation of the site from third century BC to the fourth century AD (Lal, 1949: 67).

A third season of excavation was undertaken by B.K. Thapar of ASI, but the results remained largely unpublished. Thapar claimed to have excavated two megaliths between the fortified settlement of Sisupalgarh and Brahmesvara temple along the northern bank of the rivulet Gangua. A re-analysis of the excavated data indicates that the structure was a Buddhist stupa with a double circle of laterite blocks marking the circumference of the stupa supported by earth filling in the centre (Ota 2007, 72-73). More recent excavations have suggested that the dates be pushed back by two centuries and that the site continued until the seventh century (Mohanty and Smith 2008).

Although the *Puranas* and other texts often refer to Bhubaneswar as *ekamra-ksetra*, famous for worship of Shiva, there is no denying that several Buddhist centres flourished in and around the present city of Bhubaneswar. The colossal *linga* of Bhaskaresvara temple is thought to be a part of an Asokan pillar (Figure 2.5).

A bell capital was found in a tank near the Ramesvara temple and railing pillars dug up near the Bhaskaresvara temple indicate the existence of a stupa (Figure 2.6 and 2.7). Finds of images of the Buddha, Avalokitesvara, Tara and Cunda, dated from eighth to eleventh centuries in the vicinity of Bhaskaresvara and Brahmesvara temples and now kept in the Orissa State Museum (Figure 2.8, 2.9 and 2.10), indicate that many of the early monastic centres at Bhubaneswar continued well into the medieval period (Donaldson 2001: 48).

Fig. 2.6. 1st century BC railing pillar found at Bhubaneswar and now in the Orissa State Museum.

Thus, it is evident that in the third century BC, the Buddhist religious landscape came to be defined through a series of monumental remains, such as pillars, edicts on

Left:
Fig. 2.7. Railing pillar from Badagada, an erstwhile suburb of Bhubaneswar.

Right:
Fig. 2.8. 8th century image of Tara from Bhubaneswar.

rock and Buddhist stupas. Though there are references in the Pali Canon to donations of buildings and residences to the Buddhist Sangha, there is little archaeological evidence for these before the Mauryan period. In recent years, many of the sculptural vestiges of these early stupas are recreated in more modern constructions.

A major sponsor for the setting up of Buddhist stupas based on earlier models is the order of Nipponzan Myohoji founded by the Venerable Nichidatsu Fujii (1885-1985). Fujii first came to India in 1931 and was later closely associated with Mahatma Gandhi. He decided to set up *Shanti* Stupas or 'peace pagodas' in order to develop programmes for promoting peace and non-violence and eighty of them have so far been established worldwide, of which six are in India. A white *Shanti* Stupa was built close to the summit of Dhauli hill by the Japan Buddha Sangha and the Kalinga Nippon Buddha Sangha in the 1970s

(Figure 2.11). When and how were the edicts discovered? Did scholars understand the language of the inscriptions at the time of discovery? We will discuss these issues with specific reference to Odisha in the next section.

THE DISCOVERERS

It is not clear when the knowledge of the Brahmi script used for the inscriptions of Asoka was forgotten. In the seventh century, the Chinese pilgrim Xuanzang who travelled to several sites in India associated with the Buddha claims competence in understanding the contents of the epigraphs. He is known to have visited Odra, identified with Odisha, where he found one hundred Buddhist monasteries and a large number of monks. He described ten Asokan stupas in the region, where the Buddha is said to have preached and refers to Pushpagiri monastery in the southwestern part of the region. His readings of the Asokan edicts, however, do not match with present renderings provided by scholars and it would seem that Xuanzang drew his understanding from oral traditions,

Left:
Fig. 2.9. 10th century image of the Buddha from Bhubaneswar.

Right:
Fig. 2.10. 10th century image of Tara from Bhubaneswar.

Fig. 2.11. Shanti stupa on Dhauli hill.

which had preserved a connection between the Mauryan king and the edicts. It is also curious that during his stay in coastal Odisha, the Chinese pilgrim saw "at a great distance the glittering rays of the precious gem placed at the top of the Stupa of the Tooth of Buddha; its appearance [was] like that of a shining star in space" (Wriggins, 2004: 141). This account undoubtedly referred to the stupa of the Tooth Relic in Sri Lanka, which he later visited.

Many of the archaeological discoveries in the nineteenth century were made by military officials during the course of surveys or on a search for the country's mineral resources. Lt. Markham Kittoe (1808–53) of Bengal 6th Native Infantry, for example, was deputed by the Coal and Mineral Committee to explore the coalfields of Odisha and in the process he found early inscriptions. Kittoe had come to India in 1825 as a seventeen-year-old military cadet and had obtained employment with the Coal Committee through the help of James Prinsep.

The modern history of the edicts in Odisha started in 1837, when Kittoe discovered the rock edicts at the hill of Dhauli in district Cuttack. The inscription was chiselled on the rock face of one of the three hills overlooking the river Daya, a tributary of the Mahanadi. Kittoe also published an account of the monuments of Odisha and in 1846 was appointed Surveyor to the Government of India. The same year, James Prinsep (1799–40) who started his career in India as assay master of the mint at Calcutta and Benares deciphered the Brahmi script. On 4th of April 1838, Prinsep presented a comparative study of the edicts at Dhauli with those from Girnar in Gujarat at a meeting of the Asiatic Society of Bengal and drew attention of the audience to the missing XIII Rock Edict at Dhauli and its replacement by two Separate Edicts.

Another issue that engaged the attention of scholars was the identity of the king who had issued the edicts, as all the pillar edicts opened with the phrase: 'thus speaks Devanampiya Piyadassi'. Who was Devanampiya Piyadassi? Nineteenth century archaeologists had difficulty in identifying the king as

Fig. 2.12. ASI shed for Asokan rock edict on Dhauli hill.

Asoka and this issue was finally resolved only after the chronicle *Mahavamsa,* written in Pali in the fourth-fifth century AD in Sri Lanka, had been consulted. The *Mahavamsa* as mentioned earlier traces the history of the island from the advent of Vijaya in 483 BC to the present. Its authorship is attributed to a Buddhist monk Mahanama who wrote under the patronage of a Sri Lankan king. The Buddha himself is said to have travelled to the island and the chronicles present detailed accounts of his three visits. Asoka's concept of *Dharmavijaya* is restated in the Chronicle.

J.D. Beglar, the Armenian assistant of Alexander Cunningham (1814-93), the first Director-General of the Archaeological Survey of India, which had been set up in 1861, visited Odisha in 1874-75. He refers to a lake west of Bhubaneswar. On the western bank of the water-body he mentions two ranges of low rocky hills running parallel to each other. On the north face of the southern range is the elephant cut out of the rock, beneath which is engraved what is known as the Dhauli version of Asoka's edicts. He reiterated in his report the great veneration of the elephant by the local people. "The most solemn mode of administering the oath to witnesses in criminal trials is to make them swear 'by Dhavaleswari Mata' ", said to be the tutelary deity of Dhauli hills. Beglar mentions "the remains of a stupa on the flat terrace of the hill near the elephant, and also one facing it on the opposite ridge, but they had long ago been dug into" (Beglar, 1882: 95).

Unlike Dhauli, where the edicts were cut on the rock-face at the side of the hill, at Jaugada, the inscriptions are located on rock within an old quadrangular earthen fort, which was surrounded by a wide and deep moat. Jaugada also owes its discovery to Kittoe, though in contrast to Dhauli, it continues to be somewhat remote. The inscription is damaged and has peeled off in several places. The mud fort was nearly square with two entrances in each face and towers of earth at each corner. Though much decayed, remnants of the mud-fort still survive. Beglar excavated trenches through the fort walls, which were made entirely of earth, though two distinct strata were clearly identifiable (Beglar, 1882: 112). Mud-forts are unique to Odisha and in addition to Jaugada other examples are known, such as the one at Sisupalgarh in Bhubaneswar (Yule 2008).

Later archaeological excavations conducted at Jaugada revealed prehistoric beginnings for the site. Trenches laid on the mound and across the earthen rampart surviving to a height of 25 feet in places revealed two phases of settlement. Period I represented a full-fledged iron-using culture, while brick and stone structures were encountered in Period II. A punch-marked coin was found in the early deposits, while Puri-Kushan coins were scattered throughout Period II (*Indian Archaeology—A Review 1956-57*: 30-31). Today, the edicts are protected in glass and iron sheds (Figure 2.12) and the hill-side, especially at Dhauli, has been landscaped with grass and trees.

THE RELEVANCE OF ASOKA'S *DHAMMA*

Scholars debate almost every aspect of Asoka's reign. Nevertheless, he was a remarkable ruler in ancient India whose message of compassion has not lost its appeal. In his Major Rock Edicts, Asoka forbade the slaughter of animals in the royal kitchen and spoke of deference to elders, obedience to parents and not harming all living beings. He appointed special officers for the propagation of *dhamma* and the administration of charities. He encouraged regard for slaves and servants, respect for teachers, restraint in behaviour towards living being, and gifts and donations to sramanas and brahmanas (Guruge, 1993: 233-36).

The Mauryan Empire is seen as the first unified kingdom of the Indian subcontinent which retained centrality within different traditions of the subcontinent and, perhaps most importantly, came to be associated with the present Republic of India. A Resolution proposed by Pandit Jawaharlal Nehru and passed in the Constituent Assembly on 22 July 1947, just prior to India's Independence, accepted the choice of the *cakra* or wheel on India's national flag. Pandit Nehru expressed his gratification at the selection of the emblem and stated:

> For my part, I am exceedingly happy that in this sense indirectly we have associated with this Flag of ours not only this emblem but in a sense the name of Asoka, one of the most magnificent names not only in India's history but in world history.... Now ... the Asokan period in Indian history was essentially an international period of Indian history. It was not a narrowly national period. It was a period when India's ambassadors went abroad to far countries and went abroad not in the way of an empire and imperialism, but as ambassadors of peace and culture and goodwill (Gopal 1984: 71-2).

Therefore, Nehru continued, the flag was a symbol not of empire or imperialism, but of freedom and peace. What could be a better way, he felt, of honouring Asoka's legacy than the continuity of his symbols in post-Independence India? It is for this reason that the lion capital found on the pillar at Sarnath occurs extensively on government stationery, postage stamps, official vehicles, coins and currency notes. Asoka's voice is indeed omnipresent and speaks strongly through his edicts at Dhauli and Jaugada. What needs to be recovered is the rich oral tradition and local and regional narratives that developed around these edicts over time. It was this vibrant oral tradition that helped the edicts to survive through the centuries.

Chapter 3

Monastic Centres in Odisha

> All the topes in the entire world are of one lustre and all of them lead to heaven and emancipation; the people who are mindful of their duties should in all respects and at all times pay homage
>
> *Thupavamsa*

The worship of the stupa is a religious duty linked to spiritual emancipation, but one which also places the worshipper within the larger domain of Buddha *sasana* or teachings of the Buddha. The *sasana* permeated across ethnic and political boundaries both within the subcontinent as also beyond it. It provided identity through obligatory pilgrimage and rituals and laid the foundation of an extensive pan-Indian religious and cultural ethos. These linkages were often through routes of trade and communication, which in no way diminished the autonomy of the Buddhist Sangha (Ray 1986, 1994, 2003). The stupa formed the core of Buddhist sites in the subcontinent and was the first structure to be established. Monasteries and other structures developed around the stupa and the immediate precincts of the stupa continued to be regarded as sacred.

It is curious that the Pali *Vinaya* contains no rules, which govern the behaviour of monks with regard to stupas, nor does it define the shape and form of the stupa to be worshipped. This absence has generally been taken to mean that the construction and worship of stupas was the concern of laymen and women rather than monks and nuns. Schopen argues against this assumption based on data from inscriptions, which refer to donations by Buddhist monks and nuns (Schopen, 1997: 86-98). Learned monks and nuns termed *tripitakas* in the records set up the first cult images dated to the early centuries of the Christian Era at the sites of Sarnath, Sravasti, Kausambi and Mathura. Another sphere where monks and nuns contributed in a major way was in the construction of monastic sites, as evident from post-Mauryan inscriptions. References in early Buddhist literature, such as the second century BC *Apadana*, indicate that festivals were organized by *theras* or monks to generate resources for the establishment of stupas (Walters 1997: 170-71). This is further corroborated by the epigraphs; for example, the monks and nuns contributed nearly 30% of the donations for the stupa at Bharhut and almost 32% at Sanchi.

The *Mahaparinibbana sutta* of the Digha Nikaya recounts the last days of the Buddha and is one of the most studied texts of early Buddhism. It has been generally dated between the end of the third and the beginning of the first century BC (Trainor 1997: 47) and exists in many renditions. The text makes an important distinction between a stupa and a *chaitya*. While the former denotes a funerary monument, the latter refers to a shrine, especially at the four places associated with the Buddha's life where early shrines were built. The word *chaitya* or *vrlksa chaitya* is found in second century BC inscriptions at Bharhut, but is used to denote tree-in-railing shrines in the sculptural representations (Sarkar 1993: 4). The issue then is: when did the apsidal shrine and the stupa appear in Odisha and what form did these take?

THE APSIDAL *CHAITYA* AND THE STUPA

In the Jajpur district of Odisha are the picturesque khondalite hills, which contain extensive mounds, and a large number of Buddhist sculptures have been recovered from here since the nineteenth century. The hill quarries of Lalitgiri or Naltagiri, not very far from the south bank of the river Birupa, are an invaluable resource of stones of good quality and also presently house traditional stone-carvers who follow ancient texts. N.K. Bose used one of these texts, viz., the *Bhubanapradipa* to define and elaborate the *Canons of Orissan Architecture*. Udayagiri is located between the rivers Genguti and the Birupa.

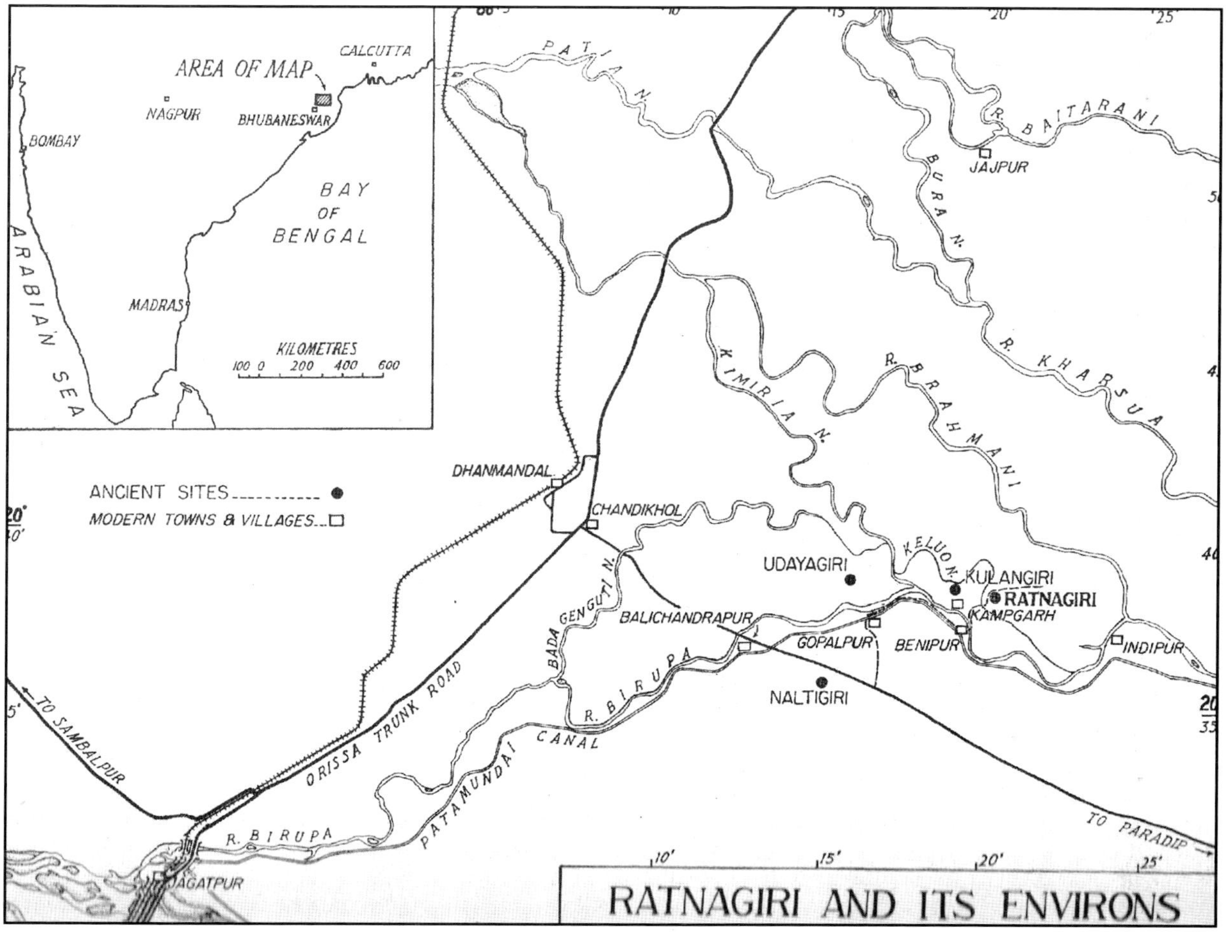

Fig. 3.1. Ratnagiri is located midway between the Brahmani and Birupa rivers. The alluvial deposits brought by the rivers have contributed to the fertility of the land surrounding the hill.

Both Lalitgiri and Udayagiri provide evidence for the presence of apsidal shrines, with Lalitgiri being the earlier of the two (Figure 3.1).

Excavations at Lalitgiri have provided evidence for a second-first century BC stupa, an apsidal shrine built over the remains of an earlier structure, inscriptions in Kushana-Brahmi, Gupta and post-Gupta script, as also a Gupta coin. A second century AD Brahmi inscription from the pavement of the apsidal shrine records the completion of a seat by several lay devotees and a nun. Also found from the site were dull red ware sherds with inscriptions dated to first century BC (*Indian Archaeology—A Review 1987-88*: 88). Forming an outer ring around the *chaitya* were small monolithic stupas, some with inscriptions of fourth-fifth century alternating with Buddha images. Though the *chaitya* at Lalitgiri dates to the second-third century, only a few images have been found dating from the early period (Figure 3.2). Relics in gold foil were found from

Fig. 3.2. Apsidal shrine unearthed during archaeological excavations at Lalitgiri.

the stupa at Lalitgiri and will be discussed in detail in the next chapter (Bandyopadhyay, 2007: 9-10).

Archaeological excavations were undertaken at Udayagiri in Jajpur district over several years, the latest being in the southern section of the valley in 2001-03. The excavations unearthed a brick-built *chaitya*, brick, monolithic and masonry stupas and a long drain made of stones for emptying water from monastery 2 and the shrine complex. The earliest structure at the site dated to the beginning of the Christian Era was a stone platform. An inscribed relic casket and Puri-Kushan coins were found in its vicinity. Around the third century AD, an apsidal *chaitya* was built on its southern side, which enshrined a masonry stupa (Figure 3.3). Around the sixth century, a brick-built shrine was raised over the apsidal structure, though the stupa was retained. The entire area underwent further changes in the tenth century when the shrine and the stupa had collapsed. A low platform was built with pedestals for setting up five colossal images of the Buddha (Trivedi 2012: 31-35).

The number of apsidal shrines of Buddhist affiliation in the subcontinent increased rapidly between the 2nd century BC and the 7th century AD. These included both rock-cut *chaityas* in the Deccan as well as structural temples with by and large Buddhist affiliation found over an extensive region from Udayagiri in Odisha (*Indian Archaeology—A Review 1958-59*: 38-40) to Sanchi in Central India and from Taxila in the north to Brahmagiri in the south. At Nagarjunakonda, the apsidal shrine with a stupa in its apse was either associated with the Mahacaitya (sites 1 and 43) or formed a part of a residential enclosure for Buddhist monks (site 38) and in the latter case no stupa was found in the

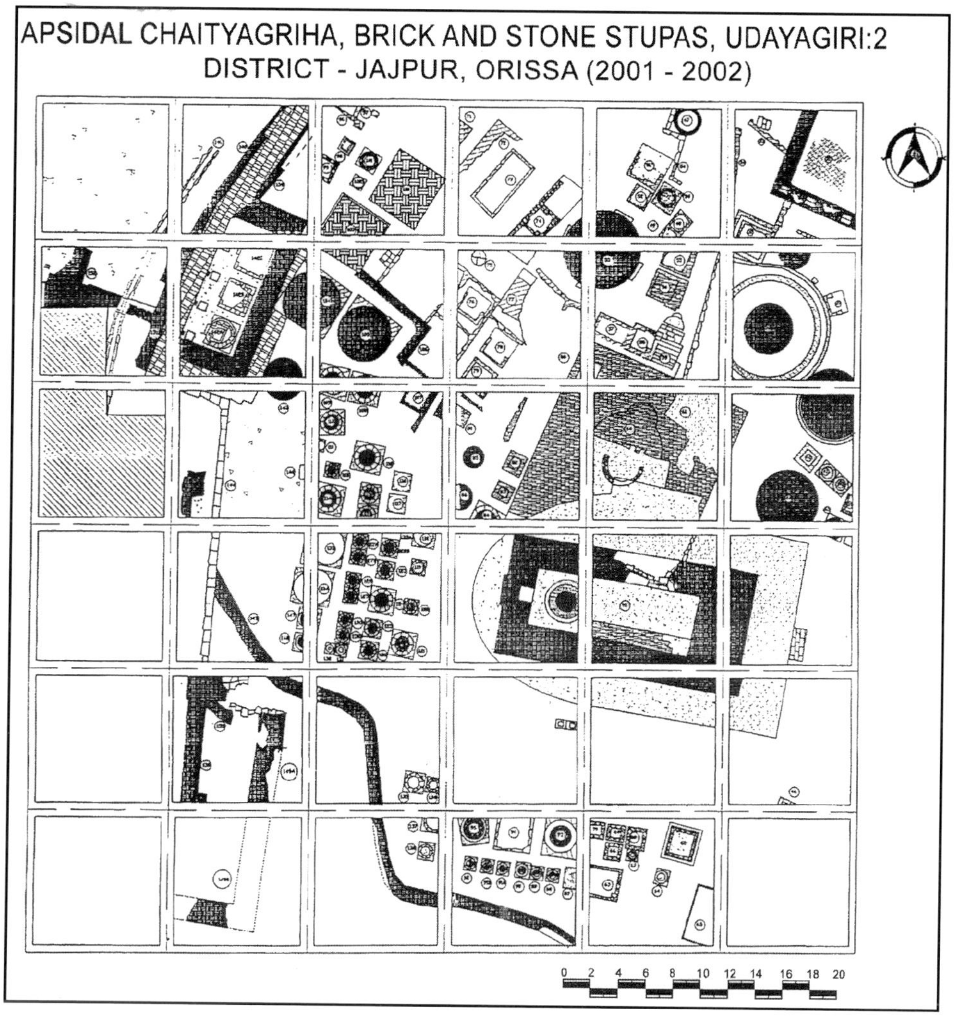

Fig. 3.3. Plan of Udaigiri 2, as a result of excavations conducted at the site from 1997 to 2001.

apse leading to the suggestion that it may have enshrined either a Buddha image or *Buddhapada* found in its vicinity (Sarkar 1993: 77-78). In another case (site 9) the apsidal shrine located near the citadel formed a part of the monastery and was meant for the image of the Buddha (Sarkar and Misra 1999: 34). Site 85 was also situated close to the southern rampart wall and the monastic complex contained two *caityagrhas*—one oblong and the other apsidal—both enshrining images of the Buddha (Sarkar and Misra 1999: 36). In contrast to the Andhra case, in Odisha, the apsidal shrine developed a distinctive outer ring of portable stupas, as mentioned earlier.

Facing Page:
Fig. 3.4. 11th century crowned Buddha from Ratnagiri, now in Patna Museum.

Dynamic artistic regional traditions evolved from eighth to thirteenth centuries at a time when manifesting divine presence played a central role in many Indian religious practices (Leoshko 2003: 18). Particularly important is the worship of the stupa from the eighth-ninth centuries onwards, which helps

Fig. 3.5. Excavated monastery at Lalitgiri.

Fig. 3.6. The area around Stupa 1 at Ratnagiri was crowded with structural as well as stone stupas.

explain the increase in the number of stupas dedicated throughout the Buddhist world. The *kriya* and *carya* tantras emphasised the maintenance and worship of stupas and identical funerary and meritorious practices were prevalent in Mahayana, Mantrayana and Vajrayana texts (Hock 1987: 109).

THE DIAMOND TRIANGLE

The major expansion of Buddhism in Odisha took place from the fifth to thirteenth century period and stupendous monastic complexes were constructed in the three hill ranges of Jajpur district, the Alti or Nalti, Assia and Mahavinayaka. The three monastic complexes form a triangle, with the distance between Ratnagiri and Udayagiri being 5.5 kilometres as the crow flies and 3.5 kilometres between Udayagiri and Lalitgiri. The latter two hills are much broader and higher than Ratnagiri. In the vicinity of Ratnagiri, the extensive Buddhist site of Udayagiri is located in the easternmost part of the Assia hills in a horse-shoe formation, while Naltagiri or Lalitgiri is not very far on the south bank of the Birupa (Mitra 1981: 7). Local tradition refers to the region being close to the sea in the past. Ratnagiri is a 25-metre-high isolated hill of khondalite formation of the Assia range bounded on three sides by the rivers Brahmani, the Kimiria and the Birupa.

The archaeology of these monastic complexes has a long history, as these sites were known since the nineteenth century. In 1869, C.S. Banerjee, the Sub Divisional Officer of Jajpur, visited Lalitgiri and wrote about the site. Over the years, several images have been removed from the area and some are now housed in museums (Figure 3.4).

Fig. 3.7. The slab with the 10th – 11th century stupa showing Buddha in preaching mudra in fairly high relief was found in the passage between monastery 1 and monastery 2 at Ratnagiri and is now in the site museum.

Fig. 3.8. Façade of the monastery at Ratnagiri made of bluish-green chlorite. At the base of the intricately carved door jambs are groups of four male figures.

A gallery of rock-cut Boddhisattvas is in evidence at Lalitgiri. R.P. Chanda (1873-1942), a pioneer in the study of Indian archaeology, recorded this when he visited the site in 1930 (Chanda 1930: 9). In 1985, the Archaeological Survey of India excavated the mound at the top of Landa hill and unearthed a stupa, which yielded three small relic caskets. Four monasteries were unearthed in continued excavations (Figure 3.5), with monastery 4 providing evidence of a shrine chamber with the image of the seated Buddha. A seal found in monastery 4 had the Sarnath sign with a *cakra* flanked by deer on top and an inscription reading *sri candraditya vihara samagra arya bhiksu sangha,* indicating that the name of the establishment was Sri Candraditya Vihara. Several pillars found from monastery 3 are similar to those from Brahmanical temples in Bhubaneswar.

The hillock of Ratnagiri is situated on the banks of the Kelua River about twenty-one kilometres south of Jajpur as the crow flies. Excavations were conducted by the Archaeological Survey of India at Ratnagiri from 1958 to

1962, which unearthed an impressive stupa surrounded by large numbers of stupas of various sizes, two quadrangular monasteries and remains of eight shrines with small temples around some of them. Varied deposits were found inside the structural stupas (Figure 3.6) and included partly charred bones, as well as reliquaries in the form of earthen vases, at least one of which contained a coin identified as a Ganga *fanam* dated to thirteenth century AD (Mitra 1981: 28, 53). Also associated with the main stupa were a large number of monolithic stupas, many of them with the Buddha or Buddhist deities carved in relief (Figure 3.7).

Monastery 1 at Ratnagiri, comprising a stone-paved central courtyard surrounded by a verandah and twenty-four cells with a shrine in the centre of one of the sides, may rank among the finest in the Indian subcontinent (Figure 3.8; Mitra 1981: 152). The shrine contained an image of the Buddha in the *bhumisparsa mudra* (Figures 3.9 and 3.10). Monastery 1 had an upper storey and indicates two phases of repair and construction. Cell 17 in the monastery housed a large number of bronze images of the Buddha and other deities, as well as metal seals and sealings reading *sri-Ratnagiri-maha-vihariyarya-bhiksu-sanghasya*. Two stone stele fixed to the eastern wall of the monastery record donations made by a *kayastha* named Janananda from the Buddhist site of Nalanda in Bihar. These included the grant of two *pravara* measures of paddy from each *hala* measure of land to the monks residing in the complex at Ratnagiri (Mitra 1981: 213-14). Ratnagiri is one of the longest lasting

Fig. 3.9. Shrine in back wall of monastery 1 at Ratnagiri. The two door jambs are elegantly carved, though the upper portions are missing.

monastic complexes in the area, as its stupa is known to have been repaired in the sixteenth century (Donaldson 2001: 57).

Ratnagiri is also remarkable for the twenty-seven metal images found during excavations, including the figure of a devotee. Of these, fifteen images were found from cell 17 of monastery 1 and comprised images of the Buddha, Bodhisattvas and Tara (Figure 3.11). The excavator, Debala Mitra, has argued on the basis of archaeological evidence that many of the images would have been produced at Ratnagiri itself (Mitra 1983: 353). Perhaps the most interesting image is that of Krishna-Yamari, also from monastery 1, but from a different part (Figure 3.12). A finely crafted specimen of the late ninth and early tenth century, the image represents a male wrathful meditational deity of the Anuttarayoga class of Vajrayana literature.

Though Buddhist remains from Udayagiri on the river Birupa were first recorded in 1870, it was only in 1985 that large-scale excavations were undertaken at this extensive site, which in many ways is different from that of Ratnagiri. At the base of the hill is a rock-cut well with thirty-one steps leading down to the water (Figure 3.13 and 3.14). A tenth-eleventh century inscription in the rock records that it was dedicated by Ranaka Vajranaga (Chanda 1930: 10). It was from this area that an exquisite door frame was discovered, which is now displayed opposite the entrance of the Patna museum (Figure 3.15).

Facing Page:
Fig. 3.10. 2.16 m seated image of the Buddha in shrine placed in the back wall of monastery 1 at Ratnagiri.

Fig. 3.11. Bronze image of seated Tara with one leg pendant, found in cell 17 of monastery 1 at Ratnagiri.

Excavations uncovered a stupa, an imposing monastery covering 30

Left:
Fig. 3.12. An excellent example of the late 9th and early 10th century, the bronze Krishna-Yamari image in the round was found in front of cell 18 at Ratnagiri.

Right:
Fig. 3.13. Step-well at Udayagiri first described by Chandra Sekhar Banerji, Deputy Magistrate of Jajpur, who visited the site in 1870. The tenth – eleventh century inscription reads 'This well (is dedicated by) Ranaka Vajranaga'.

metres square and a residential-cum-shrine complex, with a central shrine chamber housing the image of a seated Buddha in *bhumisparsa-mudra* (Figure 3.16 and 3.17), as also a massive water reservoir. Seals found from the excavations refer to the site as Madhavapura mahavihara. Near the top of the western spur of the hill overlooking the river Birupa are a series of rock-cut images of the Buddha and Bodhisattvas with a votive stupa in front. The first image is that of Avalokitesvara and bears two inscriptions. One is a popular Buddhist *dharani* and the other records that the image was a gift of Simyaka. Peculiar to Udayagiri is the alignment of the eight Bodhisattvas forming a *mandala* around a central figure (Donaldson 2001: 64).

The presence of Buddhism is most marked in the area around Langudi Hill in Jajpur district. Langudi, on a low hill running from north to south, is located in the plains of the Mahanadi Delta about 90 km from Bhubaneswar (Figure 3.18). The river Kelua, a tributary of the Brahmani, the second largest river system in Odisha, meanders across the northeast and eastern parts of the Langudi Hill. Thirty-four rock-cut stupas of varying sizes were carved in low

relief on the northern spur of the hill along with several images of *dhyani* Buddhas and Tara. Excavations conducted on the top of the hill unearthed a stupa encircled by a laterite wall and covered with burnt bricks. What were the distinctive features of medieval Buddhism in Odisha? Can the monuments be 'read' to reveal distinguishing characteristics?

Fig. 3.14. Modern temple of Mahakali near step-well at Udayagiri. During Ramaprasad Chanda's visit in 1927-28 worship was offered in the temple to a group of old images with vermillion every Thursday by a priest of the Malakara caste.

UNIQUENESS OF REGIONAL TRADITIONS

A striking feature of Buddhism in Odisha is the lack of narrative sculptures, one of the few exceptions being the *astamahapratiharya* sculpture, now in the Raghunatha temple at Solampur (Donaldson 2001: 94). Tara was a popular deity in Odisha (Figure 3.19), especially at Ratnagiri, where she is found sculpted on 99 niches of monolithic stupas. She is represented both in her seated *lalitasana* form as also in various other types described in the *Sadhanamala*.

Fig. 3.15. Exquisitely carved door frame from Udayagiri, now in the Patna museum. The doorway was seen on the mound at Udayagiri by visitors to the site in the 19th century, but was then moved to Ravenshaw College, Cuttack and later to Patna Museum.

From seventh to twelfth centuries, Tara is shown as the saviour from a variety of dangers, including shipwreck, in sculpture as also in epigraphs. An early representation occurs in cave 9 of Ellora in western India and two standing images are known from Ratnagiri. She is invoked in several inscriptions, such as the Nalanda record of Vipula Srimitra dated to the first half of the twelfth century, as also the Kalasan inscription from Java. It would then seem that though there were several similarities between contemporary sites, yet every site placed emphasis on certain images suggesting local preferences for cults and specific texts. The eleventh century manuscript of *Astasahasrika*

Fig. 3.16. Shrine at Udayagiri.

Prajnaparamita in the Cambridge University Library (MSS no. Add 1643) illustrates Buddhist images and shrines from different parts of India and four of the illustrations relate to Odisha. It is not surprising that three of these refer to images of Tara, perhaps from Banpur, while the fourth refers to the monastic complex at Kuruma (Figure 3.20), near Konarak in Puri district excavated by the Odisha State Department of Archaeology (Donaldson 2001: 25).

In her study of the inscriptions and images found at Ratnagiri, Nancy Hock has shown the wide range of texts and type of texts that were in use at the site from the seventh to the thirteenth century. She makes a distinction between Mantrayana, which relies on *kriya* and *carya* tantras and an extensive use of *dharanis* and Vajrayana tantras. The *kriya* and *carya* tantras emphasised the maintenance and worship of stupas and identical funerary and meritorious practices were prevalent in Mahayana, Mantrayana and Vajrayana texts. It is also evident that at least two tantras of the Anuttarayoga group were in use at Ratnagiri by the ninth and tenth century, though a majority of the excavated images continued to be derived from the *kriya* tantras (Hock 1987: 4).

Fig. 3.18. Rock-cut stupas on Langudi hill, which is a centrally protected site about 90 kilometres from Bhubaneswar.

Facing Page:
Fig. 3.17. Buddha image in shrine at Udayagiri.

Three inscribed texts excavated from Ratnagiri included the Mahayana *Pratityasamutpada sutra* datable to the sixth century, the *Bodhigarbhalankaralaksa dharani* and the *Sarvaprajnantaparamitasiddhacaitya nama dharani*, which extol the virtues of constructing stupas. In addition specific *dharanis* were used for placement inside stupas. A preliminary survey has shown that these *dharanis* were preoccupied with problems of death and the means of either overcoming it or of obtaining release from rebirth in hell (Schopen, 1997: 121).

Ratnagiri has provided evidence for the presence of a very large number of female images, especially those of Cunda and Tara, which sets it apart from other monastic sites in Odisha, viz. Udayagiri and Lalitgiri. Cunda does not figure in the large stone sculpture at Ratnagiri, but she is repeatedly represented on votive stupas. Fourteen examples of Cunda are known including both four-armed and two-armed forms. The two stupendous standing life-size stone images of Tara from Ratnagiri are striking. In 1927-28, Ramaprasad Chanda, an official of the Indian Museum, Calcutta visited Ratnagiri and other sites in Odisha to collect Buddhist sculptures for the museum. He found a number of sculptures near the Mahakala temple on the hill at Ratnagiri, including the *astamahabhaya* Tara image, which is now in the Patna museum (Mitra, 1981: 11). The standing image is dated to the eleventh century on the basis of a fragmentary inscription and graphically portrays the *jalarnava-bhaya* or fear of drowning in a sinking boat (Mitra 1983: 428). A second image, now in the site museum at Ratnagiri, dated to the end of the eighth century AD, shows Tara flanked by scenes of the eight perils depicted in two vertical rows of four panels each (Mitra 1983: 444-5). A third eleventh-twelfth century seated image is fixed to the outer compound wall on the outskirts of Shergarh district in Balasore district. The *astamahabhaya* form of Tara does find mention in one *sadhana* of the *Sadhanamala* text as saviour from the eight perils, though in the *Saddharmapundarika sutra* and the western Deccan caves, it is the Avalokitesvara who is revered as the saviour. Clearly the practice of Buddha *dhamma* drew not just from contemporary and earlier textual traditions, but also from requirements of communities who provided patronage to the Sangha.

It is sometimes suggested that the evolution

Fig. 3.19. The 30.6 cms image of Tara in *varada mudra,* seated on lotus originally belonged to one of the niches of the elaborately embellished stupa 16 of stone masonry and is now in Ratnagiri museum.

Fig. 3.20. Conserved monastic remains excavated by the State Department of Archaeology at Kuruma, a small village not far from Konarak.

of the esoteric form of Buddhism led to a shift from Avalokitesvara as saviour to the changed association with Tara as at Ratnagiri. Though it is often difficult to trace the precise trajectory of this complex development, the earliest of the revealed tantras, viz., the *Guhyasamaja Tantra* seems to have been compiled during the fifth-sixth centuries. From the seventh century onwards, Tantric Buddhist thought gained momentum and several Buddhist sites, such as Kanheri, Aurangabad, Ellora, as well as centres in Odisha, Bengal and Bihar reflect this form of Buddhism (Huntington and Bangdel 2003: 23-27). An emphasis on the female principle was a distinguishing feature of tantra, as also the use of sexual symbolism. Tantric metaphysical systems conceived of absolute reality in terms of non-duality of binary opposites such as male-female, right-left, sun-moon, purity-impurity, etc. The *kriya* and *carya* tantras emphasise the importance of Sakyamuni Buddha and forms of Bodhisattvas, such as Avalokitesvara and Tara. The Buddhist pantheon expanded and there is increased appearance and importance of female imagery.

Over the last few decades, there have been attempts at identifying specific texts that may have been used at Buddhist monastic sites, both in India and elsewhere. For example, A. Ghosh published the text of an inscription found on a stone slab (now in the museum at Cuttack) and also presented similar texts found on terracotta tablets from Nalanda written in Nagari characters dating from sixth to ninth century AD, as well as those from Paharpur and Bodh Gaya. Though Ghosh was unable to identify the text, it is now evident that the stone slab represented a short Sanskrit version of texts preserved in the Tibetan Kanjurs. Texts such as the *Bodhigarbhalankaralaksa* and *Vimalosnisa* form a group of texts that were widely known and used for inscribing *dharanis* on terracotta plaques not only at sites in Odisha, but across the Buddhist world in Tibet, China as well as Sri Lanka. This led Schopen to conclude:

> If by 'tantric' we mean that phase of Buddhist doctrinal development, which is characterized by an emphasis on the central function of the guru as religious preceptor; by sets – usually graded—of specific initiations; by esotericism of doctrine, language and organization; and by a strong emphasis on the realization of the goal through highly structured ritual and meditative techniques, then there is nothing at all 'tantric' about these texts. They are texts dealing with ritual forms open to all and religious problems common to all—monks, nuns, laymen and women. Second, they show a marked continuity in terms of religious concerns with the literature that preceded them. They are, like much of the canonical Mahayana *sutra* literature that came before them, preoccupied with death and the problems of rebirth (Schopen 2005: 337).

This then raises the question of patronage and the support base of the Buddhist monastic complexes at a time when the ritual requirements of the monastic complexes had changed. The setting up of more than 700 monolithic stupas at the site of Ratnagiri itself indicates the nature of interaction between the community and the monastic complex. Linked to this is the change in the nature of grants that are now recorded. These largely record donations of land in peripheral areas and for the expansion of agriculture in coastal regions, though in some cases the beneficiaries are also religious institutions. Of a total of 340 inscriptions from Odisha dated from sixth to thirteenth centuries AD, there are references to grants made to Buddhist centres in at least fourteen cases. A copper-plate charter from Jayrampur in district Balasore dated to the first half of the sixth century AD records the grant of a village Svetabalika to the Bhikshu Sangha for constructing a vihara at Bodhipadraka (identified with present Jayrampur) for arya Avalokitesvara. The grant provided for ritual requirements of worship such as *bali*, *caru*, *gandha*, *puspa*, *pradipa*, etc. and for providing for necessities of the arya Sangha like food, bed, food, medicine, etc. (Sircar 1965: 530-31).

Several conclusions are valid at this juncture. First, that the monastic sites underwent irreversible change during the process of discovery in the colonial period and this process is crucial to an understanding of the archaeological context of the site. Second, the dynamism of the religious process associated with the setting up of the monastic centre can only be comprehended through an analysis of their historical trajectories firmly rooted as these were in regional and local cultural traditions. Finally, the stupa formed the nucleus of interaction between the monastics and the lay community and the diversity of this interaction is evident from the range of burials, cairns and memorial slabs associated with the stupa landscape.

Chapter 4

Division and Worship of Relics

> Twenty-seven years after it was excavated from the famous Lalitgiri Buddhist site, the holy tooth of Buddha will soon find its place in the state museum for public viewing.

This information was provided by the English newspaper, *The Times of India*, Bhubaneswar, on August 19, 2012 in an article titled: 'Buddha Tooth to Find Place in Odisha Museum'. The article then went on to state that this decision was taken when State Tourism Minister, Maheshwar Mohanty, took up the matter with the Director-General of the Archaeological Survey of India.

The minister further said he had also discussed with the Railways for bringing the 'Buddhist special train' called Mahaparinirvan Express to Odisha. "We plan to bring the train up to Haridaspur from where the tourists would be taken in a special bus to Buddhist sites like Ratnagiri, Lalitgiri, Udayagiri and such other places. The train, now coming from New Delhi to Bodhagaya, will soon include Odisha in its route. It will come to Odisha twice a year. Each of the trip will be of one-week duration." The minister added that the government has agreed to bear an estimated cost of nearly Rs 2.5 crore per annum for this. "We have recently written to the Railways in this regard agreeing to its condition," the minister said (*TOI*, August 19, 2012). This news item raises several issues: the first relates to the power of the Buddha's relics in archaeology and literature, which we will address in this

Fig. 4.1. Dharmarajika stupa at Taxila is a circular structure with a raised terrace around its base.

chapter. The second links the relics with the present-day demands of tourism and this will be taken up for discussion in the next chapter.

ARCHAEOLOGY OF THE RELICS

The unravelling of the story of the relics enshrined within stupas should perhaps begin with the terminology, which reflects a mingling of two significant academic traditions—the Sanskrit/ Pali tradition and its reinvention in Europe over the last 200-300 years. Thus, the Sanskrit term 'stupa' is traced to the *Rigveda* and translated as crest or summit, but in its English variant as tope it first occurs in the 1839 *Account of the Kingdom of Caubool* by Mount-Stewart Elphinstone. The Pali canon refers to *cetiya* as a shrine and it is from this that the Javanese word *candi* and the Thai usage of *cedi* derive. The Sinhalese, on the other hand, refer to the *dagaba* or *dagoba*, which has its beginnings in *dhatu-garbha* referring to the corporeal relics of the Buddha enshrined in the stupa (Cummings 2001: 42-43). In India, the term stupa or *thube* first occurs in the Nigalisagar pillar inscription of Asoka in present-day southern Nepal. According to Buddhist tradition, Sakyamuni Siddhartha Gautama was the most recent in a succession of Buddhas who have appeared on earth. This multiplicity of Buddhas was accepted by the Mauryan king Asoka in the third century BC. In the Nigalisagar pillar inscription, Asoka refers to having enlarged the stupa of Konagamana or Kanakamuni, one of the previous Buddhas. This inscription thus provides crucial evidence for an early cult of relics prevalent in the subcontinent (Strong 2004: 26).

Traditionally, the setting up of stupas in the Indian subcontinent is attributed to the Mauryan ruler Asoka, though the dating of the stupas to the Mauryan period is not corroborated by archaeological evidence. Based on the account of Asoka's patronage of Buddhism in the *Asokavadana*, Marshall credited the Mauryan king with the introduction of Buddhism into northwest India and the setting up of the Dharmarajika stupa at Taxila (Figure 4.1; Marshall 1951: 234-35).

Recent research however does not support this attribution. At Dharmarajika stupa at Taxila, for example, the earliest coins found at any of the Buddhist sites in the northwest are those of the Indo-Greek ruler Menander I (155–130 BC), thereby providing a post-Mauryan date to Dharmarajika. A majority of the coins are the square uninscribed bronze coins of the lion and elephant type dated to the second century BC. In terms of architecture, the earliest phase at Taxila is dated from 200 BC to late first century AD. It is at this time that there is evidence for the creation of public sacred areas and temples in and around the city of Sirkap, as also at the Dharmarajika complex where the earliest remains date from this period (Behrendt 2004: 7).

After the Buddha's *parinirvana,* his ashes were divided into eight parts and distributed to the eight kings in whose kingdoms he had lived and stupas constructed over these. Asoka is said to have subsequently opened seven of these and redistributed their contents over a much larger expanse of the subcontinent, thereby adding to the creation of the sacred geography. The *Mahaparinibbana sutta* refers to the distribution of the Buddha's bodily relics and their enshrinement in eight stupas, as well as the establishment of two additional stupas over the measuring box and embers from the cremation fire. These eight portions were allotted as follows (Figure 4.2): To Ajatasatru, king of Magadha; to the Licchavis of Vesali; to the Sakyas of Kapilavastu; to the Bulis of Allakappa; to the Koliyas of Ramagama; to the brahmin of Vethadipa; to the Mallas of Pava; and to the Mallas of Kusinara (Rhys Davids 1901: 397-410).

By the early centuries of the Christian Era, the narrative itself underwent transformation and expansion both temporally and spatially, as discussed by John Strong (Strong 2004: 124-49). "The tradition as a whole also gave rise to notions of miraculous images associated with Asoka, to tales of apocryphal visits of Asoka or his sons to distant lands, and to legends about Asoka's daughters. Moreover, it also served to inspire various rulers throughout East Asia who sought to emulate Asoka's paradigm for generations to come" (Strong 2004: 125).

It is striking that a distinction is evident in the earliest version of the narrative between the eight relic stupas and the four sites of pilgrimage, which do not house the bodily relics of the Buddha, such as where the Tathagata was born, where he attained enlightenment, where he preached his first sermon and where he passed away. What is of interest to this chapter is the merging of several textual traditions in the Asoka and post-Asoka periods, especially when compared with the edicts of Asoka. The proliferation of stupas across the subcontinent is phenomenal. How is this expansion in the sphere of Buddhist structural activity to be explained? How are the new regions to be incorporated into Buddhist sacred geography? Clearly, Asoka's religious activities acquired new meaning.

The second century AD *Asokavadana* elaborates the story of the eight stupas and credits Asoka with collecting the relics from the drona stupas and re-enshrining them into 84,000 stupas throughout Jambudvipa (Strong 1983: 109). Unlike the *Asokavadana*, the Sri Lankan Chronicle, the *Mahavamsa* refers to 84,000 monasteries or viharas, which Asoka established to honour the Buddha's teachings, omitting all reference to any breaking in of stupas. What is the significance of the number 84,000? Rhys Davids refers to an early verse in the Canon attributed to Ananda, which mentions that the number of sections of the *Dhamma* was 84,000, and to the *Dipavamsa*, which states that the number of Asoka's buildings was determined by the number of sections of the *Dhamma*. While the *Asokavadana* merely announces that Asoka celebrated a festival of relics on completion of his construction of 84,000 stupas, the

Fig. 4.2. Division of the relics, Gandhara 1st-2nd century AD, now in the British Museum, London.

Mahavamsa provides graphic accounts of Asoka's participation in the festivities, lavish gifts given to the Sangha, streets adorned with strings of lamps and garlands of flowers and music being played, as also sermons preached (Geiger 1912: 41).

It is apparent that by the second century AD, several new phenomena had appeared: first the Buddhist *Dhamma* had spread beyond the area that the Buddha had preached in, viz., large parts of North India to encompass both the northwest and eastern regions of the subcontinent and also to Sri Lanka. The worship of relics over this extensive area was striking, as also the proliferation in the number of stupas and monasteries that had been constructed.

A graphic representation of the division of the relics is provided by the three architraves on the gateways to the main stupa at Sanchi in Central India dated to the early centuries AD. The representations on the south (rear side, bottom architrave) and west gateways (rear side, top and middle architraves) show the siege of Kusinagara where the Mallas are said to have taken possession of the relics; the division of the relics by the Brahman Drona; and the transport of the relics by the other claimants (Mitra 2001: 38-9). The *Mahaparinibbana sutta* of the *Dighanikaya* preserves an account of the Buddha's cremation, while Buddhaghosa's commentary adds the narrative about the conflict between Ajatasatru and the Mallas over the Buddha's relics. The matter was amicably resolved after the intervention of the Brahmana Drona.

Recent scholarship asserts that the *Mahaparinibbana sutta* (*Dighanikaya* 16, 6: 23-28) indicates that the "authoritative Theravada tradition both affirmed the value of relic veneration and at the same time cautioned that it should not be the primary preoccupation of members of the Sangha" (Germano and Trainor 2004: 10). In the beginning, the relics involved were corporeal relics of the Buddha himself. Gradually, the scope was enlarged and by the beginning of the Christian Era not only the bone relics of the monks were included but also precious objects such as gold, silver, pearls, crystal, lapis lazuli and so on.

Among the most famous relic finds in India are those made at Piprahwa, a site identified with Buddha's hometown of Kapilavastu. At Vaishali, relics were unearthed from what was possibly one of the original eight stupas built over the Buddha's remains (Sinha and Roy 1969); and near Peshawar where a magnificently embossed gold reliquary was found in which there were three small fragments of bone that "are undoubtedly the original relics deposited in the stupa by Kanishka which Xuanzang tells us were relics of the Buddha" (Spooner 1908-09: 49). Sometimes the urns are specifically labelled with inscriptions identifying them as containing the remains of particular Buddhist saints or even the Buddha. Alternatively, they remain anonymous. Usually, in addition to bits of bone, the reliquaries contain such things as beads, pearls, coral, semi-precious stones, jewellery, bits of gold, silver, coins, etc. (Strong 2004: 13).

On the basis of a tradition recorded by Xuanzang, the Buddha is said to have demonstrated to his two disciples Tapussa and Bhallika, who are said to have travelled from Odisha, the proper method of setting up of a relic monument by piling up his robes folded in squares (Beal 1981/1884: I: 47-48).

ARCHAEOLOGY OF LALITGIRI

Buddhism has come to be studied in chronological terms such as Hinayana, Mahayana and Vajrayana, which are often seen as exclusive blocs or sects, generally in sequence. Recent research by Peter Skilling has convincingly shown that the term 'Theravada' itself, indicating a 'kind of Buddhism', was a nineteenth century creation. Theravada is a term rarely found in early Buddhist texts and histories or in Early European writings. Pali and Sanskrit texts refer to *acaryavada* or *nikayantara* when referring to other schools or religious affiliations (Skilling 2009: 61-94).

The archaeological treasures of Lalitgiri were first brought to notice in 1869 by Chandrasekhar Banarjee leading to subsequent documentation of the site by R.P. Chanda in 1927-28. Considering its archaeological importance, the ancient vestiges were declared centrally protected in 1937.

In 1985, the Archaeological Survey of India started excavations on a hemispherical mound on the northern side of the hill and unearthed a stupa that had been built on the hillock without elaborate foundations. Made of rubble masonry, the stupa was 15 metres in diameter and was veneered with dressed sandstone (Figure 4.3). Around the stupa was a 3-metre wide well-paved circumambulatory path. The stupa yielded two relic caskets. The khondalite casket placed in the south did not contain any relic, while the other had steatite, silver and gold caskets within each other (Figures 4.4 and 4.5).

Facing Page:
Fig. 4.3. Stupa at Lalitgiri excavated by the Archaeological Survey of India.

Fig. 4.4. Relic casket from stupa at Laltigiri.

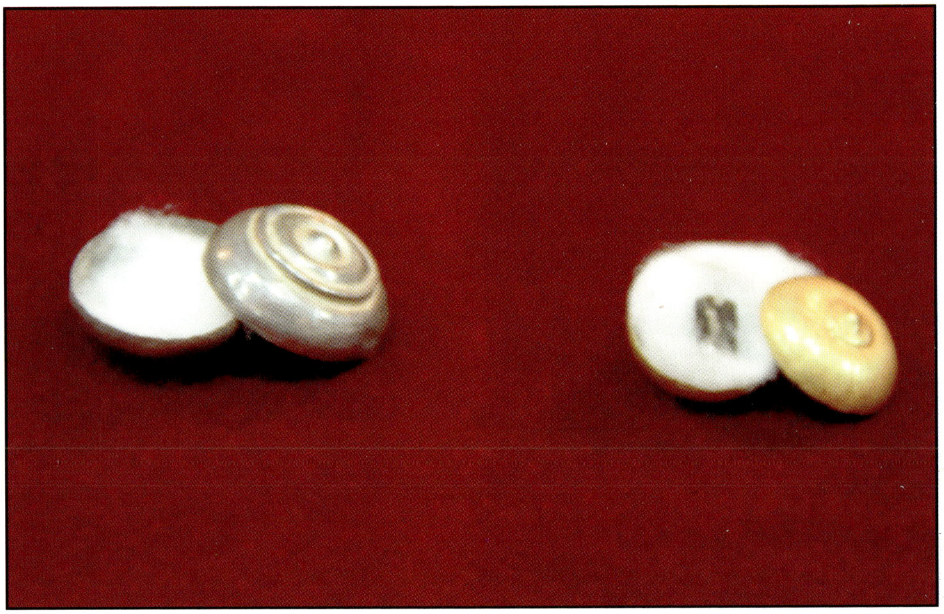

Fig. 4.5. Relics in gold foil from stupa at Lalitgiri.

The small piece of bone was kept in the gold casket (*Indian Archaeology—A Review 1985-86*: 62-63). Continued excavations at the site unearthed a huge brick-built apsidal *chaitya*, as discussed in Chapter 3, as well as four monastic complexes and several images. Peter Skilling assesses an extensive range of textual discussions of relics and concludes that the "cult of relics is central to all Buddhisms" and links the history of Buddhism to the history of relics (Skilling, 2005: 269-332).

A comparison with the hill at Sanchi in Madhya Pradesh may not be out of place. In search for relics, Alexander Cunningham visited Sanchi (Bhilsa topes) situated on a low ridge on the banks of the river Betwa and dug shafts through the centre of the stupas in January and February 1851 along with F.C. Maisey. The hill around Sanchi was marked by distinct groups of stupas within a ten kilometres radius. For example, Sonari, Satdhara, Bhojpur and Andher and many of stupas at these sites provided a rich hoard of relics. He found relics of the Buddha's disciples Sariputta and Mogalana, as evident from the inscriptions inside stupa 2 at Satdhara and stupa 3 at Sanchi. The number of inscribed relics found at Sanchi is striking and may be identified with Buddhist monks and teachers. Not all stupas, however, contained relics and Cunningham lists several that he opened without any results (Cunningham, 1854: 211-20).

This raises the issue of the landscape around the stupa, rather than focussing narrowly on the stupa itself and the search for relics.

THE SACRED MEMORIAL LANDSCAPE

The stupas enshrined relics of the Buddha and his disciples, while the space around them was often dotted with smaller structures dedicated to the monastic dead. Schopen has elaborated that, "an old literary tradition exists which indicates that the Buddha was thought to be actually present at certain spots with which he was known to have had direct physical contact" (Schopen 1987: 193-225). This physical presence of the Buddha was invoked both by monks and nuns, as also by the laity as our examples from Odisha show. Buddhist literature also contains instructions to monks to perform funeral rites for a fellow monk and to build stupas for deceased members of their community (Schopen 1997: chapter IX).

In addition to the regional variations in the sanctity of monastic sites, there is another important feature of the landscape, viz., the location of monuments to the monastic dead. As early as 1854, Cunningham published the results of his cursory excavations at Sanchi where it was clear that an extensive cemetery was associated with the Buddhist monastic site at Bhojpur and both here and at Sonari and Andher, there was evidence for the elaborate housing and worship of the monastic dead. Similarly, at Bodh Gaya hundreds and thousands of small stupas of various sizes were crowded in a jumbled mass around the central point of the site.

More than seven hundred portable monolithic stupas were exposed in the area around the monastery at Ratnagiri and by their sheer numbers these indicate that the site competed with Bodh Gaya (Mitra 1981: 31). Five hundred and thirty-five of the portable stupas were found on the southwestern side of the main stupa area and date from the ninth to thirteenth century AD. Of these, 269 stupas have a single niche with the image of a deity enshrined within it, while one has two niches. The most popular deity was Tara followed by the Buddha, Avalokitesvara, Manjusri, Marici and Vajrasattva. "These stupas were evidently raised by devotees who intended to earn merit by installing them near the main stupa" (Figures 4.6 and 4.7; Mitra 1981: 27) and the deities enthroned in the niches of stupas may indicate personal devotional images

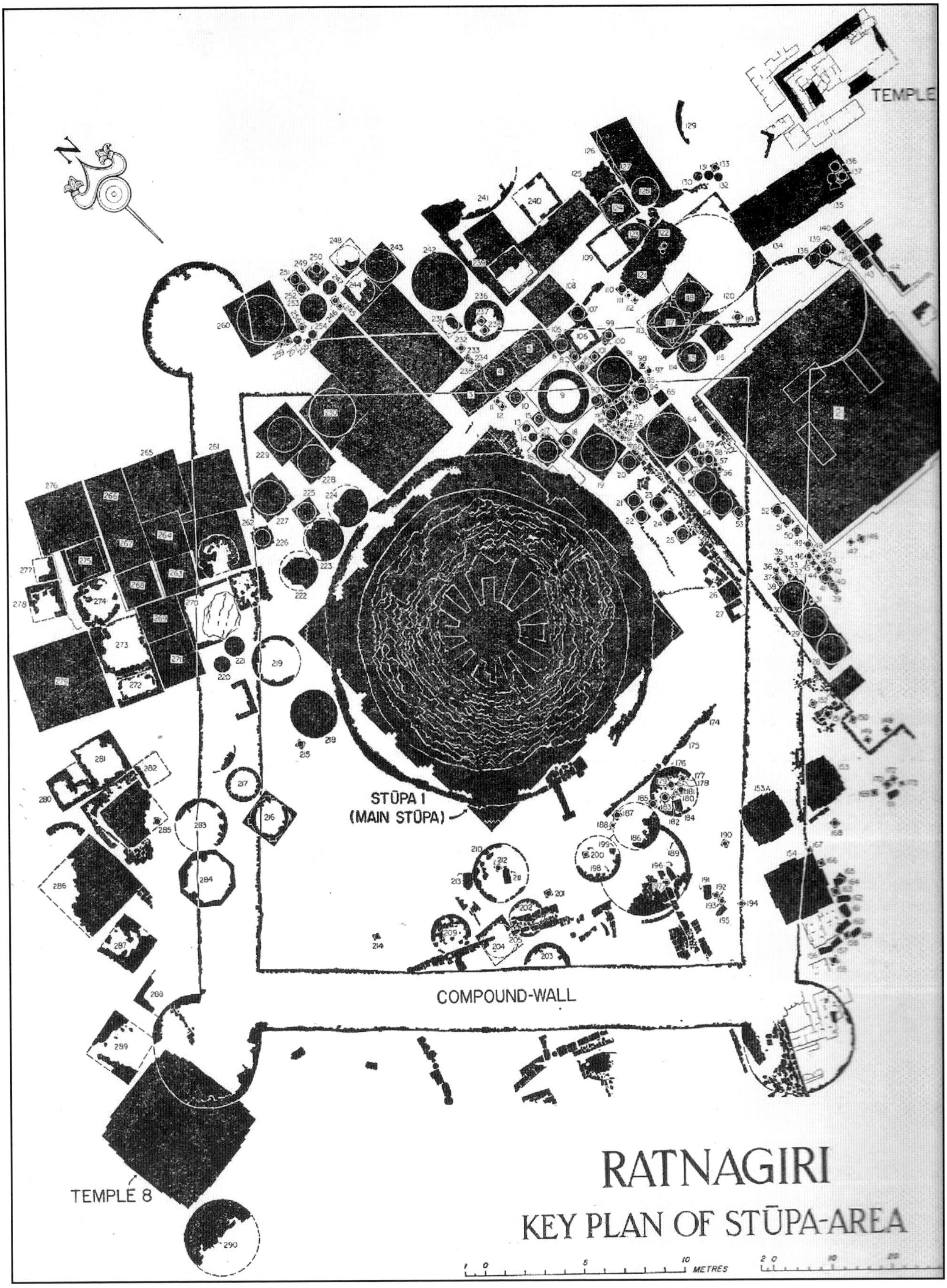

RATNAGIRI

KEY PLAN OF STŪPA-AREA

Fig. 4.7. Monolithic portable stupas form an interesting group at Ratnagiri and were used for enshrining relics, stone and terracotta tablets.

chosen for the monk or layman whose remains were deposited in the reliquary (Mitra, 1983: 112).

Hock argues for a change in style from the seventh-eighth century undecorated monolithic stupas found at Lalitgiri to the more ornate ones at Ratnagiri with a Buddhist figure in the niche. Though Cunda as a goddess does not find frequent representation in stone sculptures at Ratnagiri, she is depicted repeatedly on the monolithic stupas and seems to have been popular not only in Odisha, but also at other sites, such as Ellora in western India and Candi Mendut in Java (Hock 1987: 116).

Some of the portable monolithic stupas found at Ratnagiri were meant for enshrining bone relics, as evident from the provision of sockets at the base. This was also the case with a large number of the minor structural stupas, which yielded partially charred bones and reliquaries. The reliquaries were generally plain earthen vases or stone blocks with sockets. In some cases (for example, stupas 23, 24, 25, 62 and 115), gold beads and gold coins were also

Facing Page:
Fig. 4.6. The first season of excavation concentrated on the top of the hill and unearthed a large number of stupas as shown in the plan of Ratnagiri stupa and the area around it.

Fig. 4.8. Portable and structural stupas at Udayagiri.

Facing Page:
Fig. 4.9. Stone stupa at Udayagiri.

found. A second category of deposits consisted of inscribed stone slabs, terracotta plaques and tablets. The inscriptions consisted of the *Pratityasamutpada sutra* along with the *nirodha* section, Buddhist creed and *dharanis* (Mitra, 1983: 28-30). The *dharanis* had funerary associations, as is evident not only from the texts themselves, but also by the fact that they were found inside small monolithic stupas (Schopen 1997: 122).

Another monastic complex that has provided evidence for the presence of portable stupas is the site of Udayagiri, where three major groups of stupas were placed around the apsidal *chaitya* described in Chapter 3 (Figure 4.8). The khondalite stupa 31 was perhaps the most elaborate with deep niches housing large detachable images of Buddhist deities (Figure 4.9; Trivedi 2012: 36).

The variety presented by the stone and masonry portable stupas is striking. In contrast to Ratnagiri, excavations at Udayagiri yielded more than five hundred terracotta sealings with the *Pratityasamutpada sutra* inscribed on them. Some of them are well-baked, showing a brick-red colour, while others are badly fired (Trivedi 2012: 201-61). It is also important to note that excavations at Udayagiri yielded an inscribed relic casket, but no further information is available on the relics.

These unbaked clay seals and sealings are ubiquitous at Buddhist sites in the early medieval period and in nineteenth century literature were often wrongly described as pilgrim's mementoes. Instead, they are ritual objects associated with merit-making. Based on descriptions provided by Xuanzang, it is evident that the production of sealings was linked to merit-making and cleansing of sin. To produce an image of the Buddha or to produce a stupa brought merit. Miniature stupas and images were produced in large numbers and were ceremonially placed inside relic chambers of stupas, which were then sealed. This is an extraordinary practice, which can help trace itineraries of ritual or the circulation of cults and ideas.

This practice, it would seem, originated in north India and spread to other parts of Asia. The mass production of sealings was a ritual practice for making merit and was produced by monks, nuns, laity, kings and queens. It was a practice that cut across the different *nikayas* (Skilling, 2005).

Based on the *Mulasarvastivada Vinaya*, known from Buddhaghosa's fifth century commentary and later translations in Chinese and Tibetan, Schopen asserts that the performance of death rituals for fellow monks, negotiating ritual privileges, control of sacred relics and economic resources characterised institutionalised Buddhism of the first to fifth century AD. Monastic funerary rituals involved removal of the body, honour of the body, including bathing before cremation and recitation of sacred texts. Another aspect of these rituals was lay participation and claim to monastic relics. At this point the text categorically states that laypersons can build stupas for the relics of the monastic dead, but all such stupas should be built within the monastic complex and hence remain under monastic control (Schopen 2004: 98-106).

Facing Page:
Fig. 4.10. Portable stupas around apsidal chaitya at Lalitgiri.

The above survey accentuates the intra-site distinctiveness of the Diamond Triangle. The stupa at Lalitgiri, located on the summit of Landa Pahar, is so far the sole repository of relics in Odisha, while the core of the funerary landscape

at the site seems to be the slopes of the hillock and the apsidal *chaitya* (Figures 4.10 and 4.11). This is also the pattern at Udayagiri.

In Chapter 3, we have discussed the evidence for the longevity of the apsidal *chaitya* at the site and its surrounding space dotted with portable stupas. In contrast, the commanding presence of the stupa on top of the hill at Ratnagiri is unmistakable, as also is the dense cluster of portable stupas around it. These characteristics make each of the three major sites unique and highlight the need to preserve this singularity.

Facing Page:
Fig. 4.11. Portable stupa at Lalitgiri.

Chapter 5

Challenges of Preservation

The chapters so far have emphasized the distinctive features of the monuments of Odisha, especially its Buddhist monuments recovered in a majority of cases through archaeological excavations in the post-Independence period. We have also discussed the larger linkages of these monuments both within a pan-Indian, as also the east coast network. Cultural and religious diversity has been the defining feature of the Indian subcontinent and this is also emphasized by its built heritage. Expanding cities and homogenization of urban design and form seriously threaten the plurality of the cultural fabric that the archaeological heritage represents. In the final chapter we will address the issue of preserving this unique heritage for future generations and the challenges faced in this process.

The foundational assumptions of what and how to conserve have undergone changes in recent years, as attention has shifted from the monument to its context, both local and regional. This shift has meant the acceptance of an enlarged value system incorporating cultural landscapes and settings, living history, community involvement and the intangible heritage. Cultural heritage thus includes oral traditions and expressions; performing arts; social practices, rituals and festive events; knowledge and practices concerning nature and the universe; and traditional craftsmanship. Clearly, a landscape is a cultural construct closely linked to issues of identity, sense of place and memories.

This is further emphasized in the United Nations Educational, Scientific and Cultural Organization (UNESCO) Convention on Cultural Heritage passed at its 32nd meeting in Paris on 17th October, 2003, which focused on the intangible cultural heritage. The Convention came into force on 20th April 2005 and has been ratified by 143 countries, including by India. As a signatory to the UNESCO convention, the Government of India is obliged not only to safeguard and protect the intangible cultural heritage of the country, but also to include it in its national policy, as well as to launch schemes for education, capacity-building and creating awareness.

Fig. 5.1. High-rise buildings near Mukteswar temple at Bhubaneswar.

In many cases, monuments are located in areas of high urban pressure and under constant threat from expanding populations and creation of residential and commercial spaces (Figures 5.1 and 5.2).

Urban planners strive to introduce specific legislation and incentives for heritage zones and for the protection of heritage buildings, which are different from our concerns, viz., centrally protected monuments. In many cases the demarcation of heritage buildings becomes a restrictive rather than an enabling exercise. The Mumbai City Development Plan 2005-2025, for example, traces the history of the city of Mumbai only to the last three hundred years and identifies the built heritage of the city as those

Fig. 5.2. Modern construction around Rajarani temple at Bhubaneswar.

structures built in the nineteenth and early twentieth century (http://www.mcgm.gov.in/irj/go/km/docs/documents/MCGM%20Department%20ListCity%20EngineerDeputy%20City%20 Engineer%20(Planning%20and%20Design)/City%20 Development%20Plan/Heritage%20Conservation.pdf accessed on 9th March 2013). Unfortunately, this focus on 'heritage' leaves out centrally protected monuments such as the Jogeswari caves, Parel Siva image and so on. Clearly, sustainability has to be framed not only through a heritage agenda, but more importantly by preserving cultural rootedness of built spaces. Monuments derive value from the spatial qualities of their surroundings rather than from individual structures. It is important to realize that the best way to protect a monument is by demarcating a buffer zone around it and regulating human activity within it. It is simply not enough to plan for growth in a city based on heritage or environmental issues; development has to be monument centric.

Monument-centric expansion requires not just urban-planning and identification of heritage structures, but more importantly comprehension of the context of monuments both historical and contemporary. Historically, land near the monuments was donated and given to groups of people who were responsible for the maintenance and preservation of the structure, be it a monastery, temple, mosque, tomb or church. Land and villages were a religious shrine's precious resource. This symbiotic relationship between the local community and the shrine was eroded with the introduction of new legislation during the rule of the East India Company, as it sought to rationalize revenue collections from lands owned by religious establishments. In many cases land was redistributed leading to settlements of people who had very few connections to the religious architecture (Ray, 2012: 69-84). In other cases, especially as religious sites were abandoned or fell into disuse, the mounds developed oral traditions and narratives that sought to explain these to existing inhabitants.

Fig. 5.3. Buddha image kept under a shed and worshipped as village deity in Kuruma.

Alexander Cunningham, the first Director-General of the Archaeological Survey of India, was an indefatigable traveller who visited a large number of Buddhist sites in North India and assiduously collected stories and narratives from villagers that helped explain the Buddhist past of the village in terms of the present. These narratives are fascinating accounts of communities relating to the presence of mounds and brick remains in their villages within their own world-view of tyrants and vicious sisters-in-law, as for example in the case of the Buddhist sites of Punjab (*Archaeological Survey of India—Report of a Tour in the Punjab in 1978-79*: 69). The legends and stories relating to Buddhist sites are as diverse as the sites themselves. For example, Manikyala, located northwest of Rawalpindi, was the first stupa to be discovered by Europeans and excavated in April 1830. The remains at the site consisted of a stupa, south of the modern village, fourteen smaller buildings of the same kind, fifteen monasteries and many isolated massive stone-walls. Local tradition regarded Manikyala as the resting place of Sikandar's horse, Sikandar being the hero of the epic poem, the *Shahnameh* (Book of Kings) of Ferdowsi (935-1020).

This is also true for sites in Odisha, such as Kuruma located 7.5 km from the World Heritage site of Konarak where a 9th-10th century image of Heruka is worshipped by villagers as that of Yama, the Hindu god of death (Figure 5.3).

Beglar narrates the following story about Jaugada fort and the sati-stone inside it:

> Tradition ascribes the erection of the fort to Raja Kesari. It says that the fort was made of lac in order that cannon-balls and missiles discharged against it should be held within it by the tenacious nature of the lac and not injure the defendants either by passing through or scattering fragments of the rampart around. It is said that the Raja of this fort had a dispute with the Raja of Raolapalli, now a small village about 3 miles south-east and on the banks of the Rishikulya, who accordingly came down and besieged the fort. The defendants were by no means afraid, as they were quite confident in the strength and peculiar virtues of the lac walls of their fort in which each missile burying itself only rendered it stronger. Long the enemy sat round the fort without being able to breach the walls. One day a milkwoman came within the enemy's lines to sell milk, it is said oddly enough from within the fort but the soldiers, instead of paying her for her milk, seized it without payment. The indignant milkwoman exclaimed- 'Oh! Brave warriors, you are ready to oppress a poor woman, and call yourselves men; if you are men indeed, why don't you take the fort, which is so easy of capture?' She was seized and carried to the chief who induced her to disclose the

> secret of the fort being made of lac. 'Bring plenty of fire and bellows and apply to the walls and you will soon see the walls disappear.' Her advice was acted upon immediately; fire and bellows were brought and the fort walls began to melt. Raja Kesari hearing this was in despair. He cursed the traitor who had betrayed the secret; 'May the traitor turn to stone,' he said, and repairing to the breach sword in hand was slain. The woman meanwhile was returning to the fort; when the curse was uttered she immediately turned to stone and stands to this day! The transformed woman is nothing more or less than a Sati pillar, not even sculptured into the form of a woman, now standing on the south side near the south-west gateway of the south face of the fort (*Report of Tours in the South-Eastern Provinces in 1874-75 and 1875-76*, ASI-AR, vol. XIII, Archaeological Survey of India, 1882/2000 (reprint): 112-16).

It is these accounts of involvement of the living with mounds of the dead that provide dynamism to the archaeological record. These have, however, been largely neglected in the archaeological discourse. We thus need to find answers to the question of the relevance of the past. How is the past to be defined? Is it a static past that is enshrined in history books or does the past have meaning with reference to the present? Is the past only relevant as a revenue earner for the tourism industry? Making the past meaningful to the present communities living around monuments, is perhaps the biggest challenge.

CONSERVATION STRATEGIES

There is increasing recognition that India needs to formulate a distinct set of philosophies and methodologies for the conservation of the cultural heritage. "Modern conservation theory and the international institutions which represent and promote the precepts of the profession can be traced to European origins" (Daly and Winter 2012: 40). This is nowhere more evident than in India where the Archaeological Survey of India is entrusted with the job of protection and conservation of monuments. The ASI was founded in 1861 and Alexander Cunningham appointed its first Director-General (1861–85), barely three years after colonial rule had been established in India. However, it was not always like this. In the first five decades of its existence, there was an almost total denial of protection to standing monuments within their local surroundings, which meant that in most cases the structures were dismembered and removed from their location to be displayed in museums—often against local sentiments. An example of this was the site of Bharhut in Central India.

A dilapidated Buddhist stupa of brick covered with a coat of plaster was discovered by Alexander Cunningham in 1873 at the small village of Bharhut about 12 km south of the Satna railway station. The stupa was on a low hill locally known as Lal Pahar about a kilometre and a half to the north of the village of Bharhut. At the time of its discovery, a major part of the structure had been completely destroyed and the still intact stone railing was moved to the Indian Museum, Calcutta in 1875 (Figure 5.4).

In the nineteenth century, conservation and repair, which were looked after by local governments, had formed no part of the ASI Director-General's responsibilities. Nevertheless, several concerned officers, including Rivett-Carnac, submitted two memoranda to the Asiatic Society of Bengal urging that the Society appeal to the Government of India to issue some simple administrative rules for better protection of antiquarian remains in the various provinces of the country from destruction by tourists and the still more dangerous class of tourist guides, which the tourist creates, as well as from railway ballast contractors. He gives examples of the excavations of ancient monuments for ballast for the Fatehgarh and Kanpur railways. Another of the evils he complains is of the dilettante excavator for coins and relics, who if he finds anything is almost certain to keep it to himself and never publish it ('Protection of Antiquarian Remains', *The Indian Antiquary*, April, 1879: 105-06).

This gradually changed with the passing of The Ancient Monuments Preservation Act, 1904. Under this Act, the government could acquire land for the protection of monuments under the Land Acquisition Act, 1894, and issue notifications declaring the changed status of the monument. At the time of independence on August 15, 1947, a total of 2826 monuments had been declared of national importance. In the post-Independence period, not only was the earlier list of centrally protected monuments ratified, but several new sites were added. More importantly, with the setting up of supra-national bodies such as UNESCO in 1945 and ICCROM (International Centre for the Study of the Preservation and Restoration of Cultural Property) in 1959, India became a

Facing Page:
Fig. 5.4. Railing from Bharhut in Indian museum.

signatory to several international conventions, which then had a bearing on its conservation programmes and strategies. Interestingly, the proposal to set up ICCROM was mooted and adopted at the 9th Session of the UNESCO General Conference held in New Delhi, in 1956.

Since the 1990s there has been increasing demand from countries of Asia that the particularities of the cultural heritage of the region and its rootedness in local and regional values and social contexts be taken note of. As a result, the Xi'an Declaration on the Conservation of the Setting of Heritage Structures, Sites and Areas, 2005, article 2 states:

> Heritage structures, sites or areas [...] derive their significance and distinctive character from their perceived social and spiritual, historic, artistic, aesthetic, natural, scientific and other cultural values. They also derive their significance and distinctive character from their meaningful relationships with their physical, visual, spiritual and other cultural context and settings.

This shift has also had an impact within India, where the conservation discourse has included discussion on region specific issues. The Director-General of the Archaeological Survey of India, for example, articulated an 'Indian perspective' on World Heritage sites at the International World Heritage Expert Meeting on Visual Integrity held at Agra from 6 to 9 March 2013. To what extent has this shift in policy helped change the situation on the ground? Aparna Tandon, Project Specialist at ICCROM, for example asserts:

> From the outside it seems that the Indian Government's current cultural policy is all-inclusive and that the government is determined to professionalize its 'cultural cadres'. On the official Ministry of Culture website, a citizen's charter is posted with the intent to increase transparency and public participation. Yet, the situation on the ground is far from perfect. The centralized heritage management systems with an almost exclusive focus on the buried past have alienated local communities and have broken the links between the past and the present (Daly and Winter 2012: 47).

This link between the past and the present is sought to be reconnected through the enactment of the Ancient Monuments and Archaeological Sites and Remains (Amendment and Validation) or AMASR Act, 2010, which was passed by the Indian Parliament in March, 2010. The 2010 Act provides statutory provision for 100 metre prohibited and 100 to 300 metres regulated areas around the monument, with a complete ban on construction in the prohibited area. Perhaps it is through the bye-laws envisaged under the Act that space could be created for the coexistence of both local communities and heritage. An issue on which there are no easy answers is that of heritage and its link with identity.

HERITAGE AND ISSUES OF IDENTITY

This is a theme that has been discussed in the introductory chapter and it has been argued that its characterization should be broad-based and not restricted to include only the built heritage, as is often the case. Another relevant concern is that of shifting priorities with reference to what constitutes heritage. For example, in 1868, Rajendra Lal Mitra (1823/4–91) was commissioned by the Government of Bengal at the suggestion of the Royal Society of Arts, London to obtain casts of some of the important sculptures of ancient India. Mitra's agenda at this point was to challenge James Fergusson (1808–86), an indigo merchant, who had published works on Indian architecture about the so-called Greek influence on Indian art and architecture. Mitra's publications included the two-volume work on Hindu temple architecture and sculpture titled *The Antiquities of Orissa* published during 1875–80. He suggested that the ancient monuments of Odisha were more authentic than those located in other parts of the country which had been subject to external influences. The focus, however, remained on the Hindu temple and the Buddhist monuments of Odisha did not receive much attention until well into the twentieth century.

An analysis of the list of centrally protected monuments of Odisha (Appendix) provides insights into the shifting priorities. Of the 78 protected monuments, one is a World Heritage site, i.e., the Sun temple at Konark; four are ticketed monuments; twelve are located in densely populated urban areas; while four are in rural settlements. The first monuments to receive protection in 1909 were the fifteenth century Gangadharaswami temple and Jagadiswara temple in Ganjam. The Sun temple at Konark was added to the list in 1915.

In 1921, the Asokan rock edict at Jaugada, district Ganjam, was added to the list, while Dhauli was included in 1924. The Jain caves at Udayagiri and Khandigiri acquired protected status in 1912 and in 1937 the archaeological mounds at Ratnagiri, Lalitgiri and Udayagiri were protected. The single largest

Fig. 5.5. The present village of Ratnagiri on the western slopes of the hill above the flood plain.

category of centrally protected monuments in Odisha is that of the Hindu temple. A total of 120 Buddhist sites are known in Odisha, but only eight of these are centrally protected. A majority of the sites remain unprotected. Given this traditional bias in the list towards the Hindu temple, how is regional identity to be defined? Is Buddhism only of value as a revenue earner for tourism? In Odisha, perhaps the Buddhist site with the largest number of visitors is the Shanti Stupa at Dhauli, while Ratnagiri and other Buddhist sites are located within a rural setting (Figures 5.5 and 5.6).

CHANGES IN LAND-USE

The mud forts are a unique feature of the early history of Odisha linked to the first phase of the establishment of the Buddha *dhamma*. How are these mud forts to be protected and preserved, especially when land prices are skyrocketing and illegal building activity continues unabated? This is a situation that has impacted a large number of centrally protected sites. Perhaps the one to be most severely affected is Sisupalgarh in district Khurda. The history and

Fig. 5.6. Toshali resort at Ratnagiri.

archaeology of the site has already been discussed in Chapter 2. It was declared protected on November 13, 2005. The protected limits of the monument included an area under revenue jurisdiction of five villages, viz., Shishupal, Badadhanpur, Lingapur, Raghunathpur, and Mahabhoisasan, though the ownership of the land was not transferred to the Archaeological Survey of India, but remained with the Gram Panchayat and private individuals. This has been the customary practice followed while declaring monuments as protected. Subsequently, the Government of Odisha converted the land-use from agricultural to residential leading to the large-scale construction of houses at the site. This continued construction has destroyed the site, resulting in the complete loss of valuable archaeological heritage.

In the final analysis, it is crucial that monuments and their holistic protection form an integral part of any future development. Buddhist sites are not merely indicators of the past, but provide ample opportunity for growth, both in terms of their tourism potential and with regard to regulated urban expansion. Preserving monuments and sites in context requires not just research, infrastructure expansion, but more importantly involvement of communities.

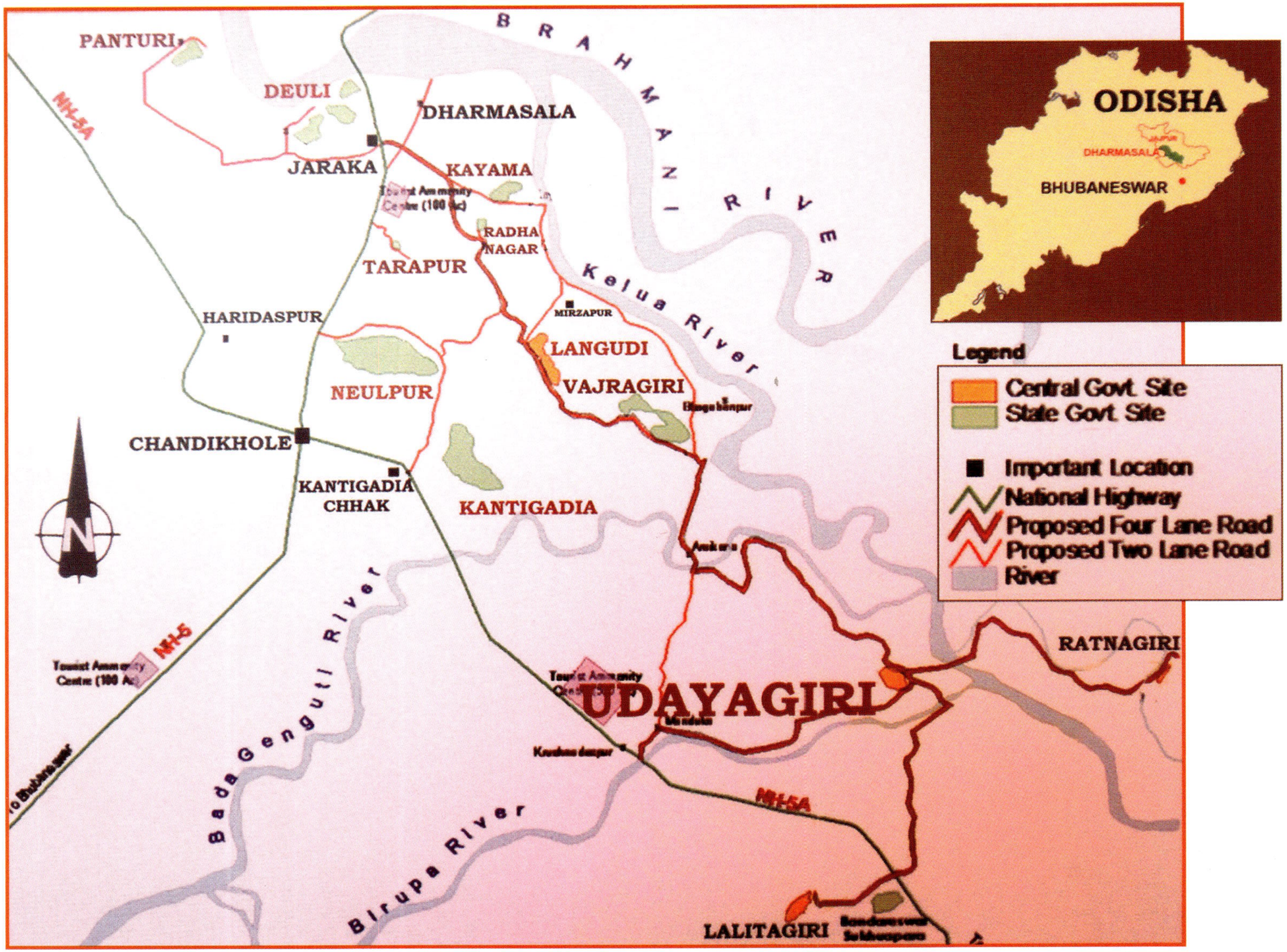

Buddhist sites of Dharmasala Area, Jajpur, Odisha.

Appendix

LIST OF CENTRALLY PROTECTED MONUMENTS IN ODISHA

Sl. No.	District	Name of site	Nature of site	Date	Notification Details
Archaeological Sites					
1.	Mayurbhanj	Baidyapur	Neolithic sites	Excavations yielding distinctive stone tools	No.5 2.1.1954
2.	Mayurbhanj	Kuchai	Neolithic site	Stone tools and pottery dtd. to 2nd millennium BC	No.5 2.1.1954
3.	Mayurbhanj	Kuliana	Palaeolithic site	Stone tools	No.5 2.1.1954
Asokan inscriptions					
4.	Ganjam	Jaugada	Asokan rock edict	On a boulder of Jaugada hillock on the left bankof river Rishikulya	MD-4425.1.1921
5.	Khurda	Dhauli (Bhuban-eswar)	Asokan rock edict and sculpture of elephant	On Dhauli hill	BO.8707-VR-21-R 10.9.1924

Sl. No.	District	Name of site	Nature of site	Date	Notification Details
Bridges and waterbodies					
6.	Puri	Puri	Bridge of 18 spans over the Madhupur stream known as Atharnulla Bridge	18th century	BO. 575-E22.3.1915
7.	Jajpur	Siriapur (Jajpur town)	Maharatta Bridge locally known as Atharnulla, also known as Tentulimal Bridge	18th century	Con.BO.2638-E 18.1.1921
8.	Khurda	Bhubaneswar	Papanasini Tank	11th – 12th century	D.5682 4.12.1985
9.	Khurda	Bhubaneswar	Sahasralinga Tank	11th – 12th century	D. 569-AR/46 30.5.1946
Buddhist and Jaina monuments					
10.	Cuttack	Lalitgiri	Ruins of Buddhist temple and images.	Apsidal caitya, stupa, vihara on hillock	OR-5215-14-3/87-Con. 20.6.1937
11.	Cuttack	Bandareswar	Ruins of Buddhist temple	9th – 10th century near Lalitgiri	OR-5213-IA/3/37 20.6.1937
12.	Jajpur	Ratnagiri	Hill containing many sculptures and images	Large monastic complex with stupa, vihara & temples from 5th–13th century	OR-5214-1A-3/37 20.6.1937
13.	Jajpur	Udayagiri	Hill containing many sculptures, images and inscriptions, etc.	Large monastic complex of 9th–10th century	OR-5214-1A-3/37 20.6.1937
14.	Jajpur	Langudi Hill	Ancient Buddhist site	Rock-cut images of 5th – 6th century	SO.No.263(E) 25.2.2004
15.	Jajpur	Ratnagiri	Dharma Mahakala Temple	16th century	SO.2995 22.9.1984
16.	Jajpur	Sub-Collectors residential complex (Jajpur Town)	Buddhist images	Images from 8th-9th to 11th century	BO.11884-VA-13-R 22.12.1924
17.	Khurda	Jagmara (Bhubaneswar)	Udayagiri and Khandagiri Caves	1st century AD	BO.2525-E 27.12.1912
Forts					
18.	Cuttack	Chaudwar (Agrahat, Bandalas, Chattisa, Govindjew Patna)	Ruins of ancient fort	12th – 13th century	OR-5217-IA-3/37 20.6.1937

Sl. No.	District	Name of site	Nature of site	Date	Notification Details
19.	Cuttack	Barabati (Cuttack)	Ancient monuments of Barabati Fort & the ruins and remains of ancient edifices, gateways, etc.	13th century fort that continued until the 19th century	BO-575 E 22.3.1915
20.	Cuttack and Khurda	Dadhapatana (Churangarh)	Churangarh Fort locally known as Sarangarh	11th – 12th century	SRC-303 Act 1954 2.11.1959
21.	Kalahandi	Asurgarh	Asurgarh Fort	3rd century BC to 5th century AD	2/8/73/M 5.3.1982
22.	Khurda	Sisupalgarh (Bhubaneswar)	Ancient remains inside and outside the ramparts	3rd century BC to 7th century AD	SR-865 13.11.1950
Hindu Temples					
23.	Angul	Bajarakote	Bhringeswar Mahadev Temple	9th century living temple of Siva	SR&CA-F4-18/60-CI 20.3.1967
24.	Angul	Rasol (Bhimakand at NTPC)	Colossal reclining image of rock-cut Vishnu at NTPC Talcher	8th-9th century sculpture in poor condition	FA/3/61/CI 5.4.1966
25.	Bolangir	Ranipur-Jharial	Chausathi Yogini temple together with three minor shrines	10th century AD	F-4-8/66-C 16.5.1967
26.	Boudh	Gandharadi	Temples of Nila-Madhava and Siddhesvara	9th century AD	SR/CA/F-4/25/60-CI 10.4.1961
27.	Boudh	Boudh	Paschima Somanatha, [Bhubanesvara] and Kapilesvara temples	10th century AD	F-4-19/63-CI 29.10.1964
28.	Cuttack	Baideswara	Durga Temple	8th century AD	F-4-39/63-CI 17.4.64
29.	Cuttack	Mugura Dhanmandal (Ganeswarpur)	Panchpandav Temple	10th–11th century AD	F-4-20/63-CI 28.4.1964
30.	Cuttack	Ragadi (Banki)	Mahimamani Temple	19th century AD	SO.No.1750 4.6.1996
31.	Cuttack	Gopinathpur	Simhanath Temple	8th–9th century AD	FA-27/16/A-CI 19.5.1965
32.	Cuttack	Padamal (Padmesvar Mahadeva Temple)	Ancient site at Banesvaranasi	8th – 13th century AD	F-4/27/64-CI 15.1.1964

Sl. No.	District	Name of Site	Nature of Site	Date	Notification Details
33.	Dhenkanal	Hatuari	Kapileswar Mahadev Temple	15th century AD	SO.No.204 (E) 17.2.2004
34.	Dhenkanal	Kapilas	Chandrasekhara Temple and group of monuments and ancient steps	14th century AD	SO.No.1358 (E) 11.12.2004
35.	Dhenkanal	Latadeipur	Annakoteswar Mahadev Temple	15th–16th century AD	SO.No.1359 (E) 11.12.2004
36.	Dhenkanal	Sarang	Colossal rock-cut reclining Vishnu	8th–9th century AD	SO.No.1361 (E) 11.12.2004
37.	Dhenkanal	Kualo	Kanakesvara Mahadeva Temple and group of temples	8th–9th century AD	SO.1360 (E) 11.12.2004
38.	Gajapati	Mahendragiri	Bhima Temple	6th century AD	Con.-MD-120 17.3.1921
39.	Gajapati	Mahendragiri	Kunti Temple	12th–13th century AD	Con.-MD-120 17.3.1921
40.	Gajapati	Mahendragiri	Yudhisthira Temple	8th century AD	Con.-MD-120 17.3.1921
41.	Ganjam	Kottakola (Buddha-Khol)	Gangadharaswami Temple	15th century AD	Con. -MD-143 25.2.1909
42.	Ganjam	Kottakola	Jagadiswara Temple	15th century AD	Con. -MD-143 25.2.1909
43.	Jagatsin-ghpur	Balia	Bhubaneswar Mahadev Temple	8th century AD	2/22/180M 4.6.1984
44.	Jajpur	Sub-Collectors residential complex (Jajpur Town)	Four colossal Maitrika images (Chamunda, Indrani, Kalijuga, Varahi)	10th–11th century AD	BO.2638-E 18.7.1921
45.	Jajpur	Jajpur Town	Jagannatha temple incld. Muktesvara Snana bedi, Bhogasala and compound wall	18th century AD	SO.800 26.2.1992
46.	Jajpur	Jajpur	Trilochaneswar Temple	11th–12th century AD	2/5/92-M 1.2.1995
47.	Jajpur	Jajpur town	Varahanath Temple	15th century AD	2/5/92-M 1.2.1995
48.	Khurda	Bhubaneswar	Bhaskareswar Temple	12th century AD	D 569-AR/46 30.5.1946
49.	Khurda	Bhubaneswar	Brahmeswar Temple	11th century AD	D 569-AR/46 30.5.1946

Sl. No.	District	Name of Site	Nature of Site	Date	Notification Details
50.	Khurda	Bhubaneswar	Nabakishore Temple	13th century AD	D 569-AR/46 30.5.1946
51.	Khurda	Bhubaneswar	Rameswar Temple	12th century AD	D 569-AR/46 30.5.1946
52.	Khurda	Bhubaneswar	Megheswar Temple	12th century AD	D 569-AR/46 30.5.1946
53.	Khurda	Bhubaneswar	Anantavasudev Temple	13th century AD	D 569-AR/46 30.5.1946
54.	Khurda	Bhubaneswar	Bakreswar Temple	14th century AD	D 569-AR/46 30.5.1946
55.	Khurda	Bhubaneswar	Vaital Deul	8th century AD	D 569-AR/46 30.5.1946
56.	Khurda	Bhubaneswar	Chitrakarini Temple	13th century AD	D 569-AR/46 30.5.1946
57.	Khurda	Bhubaneswar	Jambeswara Temple	13th century AD	D 569-AR/46 30.5.1946
58.	Khurda	Bhubaneswar	Lingaraj temple with all minor temples in compound	11th century AD	D 569-AR/46 30.5.1946
59.	Khurda	Bhubaneswar	Maitresvara temple with minor temples in compound	14th century AD	D 569-AR/46 30.5.1946
60.	Khurda	Bhubaneswar	Makareswar Temple	14th century AD	D 569-AR/46 30.5.1946
61.	Khurda	Bhubaneswar	Markandeswar Temple	8th century AD	D 569-AR/46 30.5.1946
62.	Khurda	Bhubaneswar	Muktesvara temple with minor shrines excl. Marichi Kunda	10th century AD	D 569-AR/46 30.5.1946
63.	Khurda	Bhubaneswar	Parsurameswar Temple	7th century AD	D 569-AR/46 30.5.1946
64.	Khurda	Bhubaneswar	Paramguru Temple	12th century AD	SO.4775 6.12.1983
65.	Khurda	Bhubaneswar	Siddheswar Temple	12th century AD	D 569-AR/46 30.5.1946
66.	Khurda	Bhubaneswar	Sari Deul	13th century AD	D 569-AR/46 30.5.1946
67.	Khurda	Bhubaneswar	Sisireswar Temple	8th century AD	F-4-5/64 1.7.1964

Sl. No.	District	Name of Site	Nature of Site	Date	Notification Details
68.	Khurda	Hirapur	Chausathi Yogini temple known as Mahamaya Temple	10th century AD	No.3 2.1.1954
69.	Khurda	Banapur	Dakshya Prajapati Temple	13th century AD	F.4/28/64-CI 6.12.1975
70.	Mayur-bhanj (Mayur-bhanj)	Haripur	Ruins of ancient fort and brick temples	16th–17th century AD	No.5 2.1.1954
71.	Puri	Puri	Lord Jagannath Temple	12th century AD	F.No.2/34/73-M 3.2.1975
72.	Puri	Chaurasi	Varahi Temple	10th century AD	F. 44/62-CI 14.8.1962
73.	Puri	Konark	(Sun temple) Ancient monuments of the Black Pagoda & the remains of ancient edifices, images, structures, basements, pillars, carvings, walls, gateways, etc.	13th century AD	BO. 575-E 22.3.1915
74.	Khurda	Rajarani Temple	Temple dedicated to Siva	10th century AD	BO. 2488 1.11.1913

Rock-cut cave sites

Sl. No.	District	Name of Site	Nature of Site	Date	Notification Details
75.	Jharsuguda	Vikramkhol	Rock inscription	3rd century BC	OR 5216-1A-3/37 20.6.1937
76.	Keonjhar	Sitabhanji (Danguapasi)	Rock paintings locally known as Ravana Chhaya and ancient monuments and remains	5th century AD	F-4-17/64/C-11 4.5.1964
77.	Khurda	Dhauli	Small rock-cut cell with niche and inscription of Santikara	829 AD	F-4-2/39-F&L 1.6.1939
78.	Jajpur	Siriapur (Jajpur town)	Monolithic Pillar called Chanreswar Pillar also known as Shubh Stambha	12th century AD	Con. BO 2638-E 18.1.1921

References

Anguttara Nikaya, R. Morris & E. Hardy translated, London: Pali Text Society, 1885-1910, 5 volumes.

Bandyopadhyay, B., *Udayagiri – 2*, New Delhi: Archaeological Survey of India, 2007.

Basu, N.N. 'Modern Buddhism and Its Followers in Orissa', *Archaeological Survey of Mayurbhanj,* 1, 1982, 12.

Beal, S., *Si-Yu-Ki, Buddhist Record of the Western World Translated from the Chinese of Hieun Tsiang*, first published 1884, Reprint, Delhi: Motilal Banarsidass, 1981, II.

Beglar, R.D., *Report of Tours in the South-Eastern Provinces in 1874-75 and 1875-76*, ASI-AR, Vol. XIII, New Delhi: Archaeological Survey of India, 1882/2000 (reprint): 95-8; 112- 6.

Behrendt, Kurt A., *The Buddhist Architecture of Gandhara*, Leiden: Brill, 2004.

Berkwitz, Stephen C., *South Asian Buddhism: A Survey*, Abingdon - New York: Routledge, 2010.

Bose, Nirmal Kumar, *Canons of Orissan Architecture*, Calcutta: Cosmo Publication (reprint), 1932.

Brandtner, M., 'Representations of Kalinga: The Changing Image and Geography of a Historical Region', in Kulke, H. and Schnepel, B. (eds.), *Jagannath Revisited: Studying Society, Religion and the State in Orissa,* New Delhi: Manohar, 2001: 179–210.

Chanda, Ramaprasad, 'Exploration in Orissa', *Memoirs of the Archaeological Survey of India*, No. 44, 1930: 1-23.

Chhabra, B. Ch., *Expansion of the Indo-Aryan Culture during Pallava Rule*, Delhi: Munshiram Manoharlal, 1965.

Christie, Jan, 'State Formation in Early Maritime Southeast Asia: A Consideration of the Theories and the Data', *Bijdragen tot de Taal-, Land- en Volkenkunde*, 151,2: 235-88, 1995.

Cummings, Joe, *Buddhist* Stupas *in Asia: The Shape of Perfection*, Lonely Planet Publications, 2001.

Cunningham, A., *The Bhilsa Topes*, London: Smith Elder, 1854.

Daly, Patrick and Winter, Tim, edited, *Routledge Handbook of Heritage in Asia*, London and New York: Routledge, 2012.

Donaldson, T.E., *Iconography of the Buddhist Sculpture of Orissa,* New Delhi: Indira Gandhi National Centre for the Arts and Abhinav Publications, 2001.

Fogelin, Lars, 'Sacred Architecture, Sacred Landscape: Buddhist Architecture in North Coastal Andhra Pradesh', Ray H.P. and Sinopoli, C., (eds.), *Archaeology as History in Early South Asia*, New Delhi: ICHR & Aryan Books International, 2004: 376-91.

Geiger, W. 'translated, *Mahavamsa: The Great Chronicle of Ceylon*, New Delhi: Asian Educational Services (reprint), 1912.

Germano, David and Trainor, Kevin, edited, *Embodying the Dharma: Buddhist Relic Veneration in Asia*, Albany: State University of New York Press, 2004.

Gopal, S., edited, *Selected Works of Jawaharlal Nehru*, New Delhi: Oxford University Press, 1984.

Guruge, Anand W.P., *Asoka—A Definitive Biography,* Colombo: Anand W.P. Guruge, 1993.

Hock, Nancy, *Buddhist Ideology and the Sculpture of Ratnagiri*, seventh through thirteenth centuries, PhD thesis, University of California, Berkeley, 1987.

Huntington, John C. and Bangdel, Dina, *The Circle of Bliss: Buddhist Meditational Art*, Los Angeles County Museum, 2003.

Jacq-Hergoualc'h, Michel, *The Malay Peninsula: Crossroads of the Maritime Silk Road (100 BC – 1300 AD)*, Leiden: Brill, 2002.

Kinnard, Jacob N., *The Emergence of Buddhism*, Minneapolis: Fortress Press, 2011.

Lal, B.B., 'Sisupalgarh 1948: An Early Historical Fort in Eastern India', *Ancient India*, 5, January 1949: 62-105.

Legge, James, *A Record of Buddhistic Kingdoms*, London: Sacred Books of the East, 1886/1965.

Leoshko, Janice, *Sacred Traces: British Explorations of Buddhism in South Asia*, Aldershot: Ashgate, 2003.

Lopez, Donald S., edited, *Buddhism in Practice*, Princeton: Princeton University Press, 1995.

Lowenthal, D., 1985, *The Past is a Foreign Country*, Cambridge: Cambridge University Press.

Malandra, Geri H., 1993, *Unfolding a Mandala: The Buddhist Cave Temples at Ellora*, New York: State University of New York Press.

Marshall, John H., *Taxila: An Illustrated Account of Archaeological Excavations Carried Out at Taxila under the Orders of the Government of India between the Years 1917 and 1934*, 3 volumes, Cambridge: Cambridge University Press, 1951.

Miller, Barbara Stoller, translated and edited, *Love Song of the Dark Lord, Jayadeva's Gitagovinda*, New York: Columbia University Press, 1977.

Mitra, Debala, *Buddhist Monuments*, Calcutta, 1980.

——, *Ratnagiri (1958-1961)*, Memoirs of the Archaeological Survey of India no. 80, 2 volumes, New Delhi: Archaeological Survey of India, 1981 (Volume 1) and 1983 (Volume 2).

——, *Sanchi*, New Delhi: Archaeological Survey of India, 2001 (first published 1957).

Mohanty, R.K. and Smith, M.L. *Excavations at Sisupalgarh*, New Delhi: Indian Archaeological Society, 2008.

Olivelle, Patrick, 'Asoka's Inscriptions as Text and Ideology', Olivelle, Patrick, Leoshko, Janice and Ray, Himanshu Prabha, edited, *Reimagining Asoka: Memory and History*, New Delhi: Oxford University Press, 2012: 157-83.

Omveldt, G., *Buddhism in India: Challenging Brahmanism and Caste*, New Delhi: Sage Publications, 2003.

Ota, S.B., 'Evidence of a Stupa at Sisupalgarh, Orissa: Re-interpreting Earlier Excavation Data', *Man and Environment*, XXXII, 1: 67-73, 2007.

Owen, Lisa, 'Absence and Presence: Worshipping the Jina at Ellora', Ray, Himanshu Prabha, (eds.), *Archaeology and Text: The Temple in South Asia*, New Delhi: Oxford University Press, 2010.

Page, J.A., 'A Memoir on Kotla Firoz Shah, Delhi', (with a translation of Sirat-i-Firozshahi by Mohammad Hamid Kuraishi), *Memoirs of the Archaeological Survey of India, no. 52*, 1937.

Panigrahi, K.C., *Archaeological Remains at Bhubaneswar*, 2nd Edition, Cuttack: Kitab Mahal, 1981.

Ray, Himanshu Prabha, *Monastery and Guild: Commerce under the Satavahanas*, New Delhi: Oxford University Press, 1986.

——, 'Inscribed Potsherds: A Study', *Indica*, 24, 1: 1-14, 1987.

——, *The Winds of Change: Buddhism and the Maritime Links of Early South Asia*, New Delhi: Oxford University Press, 1994.

——, 'Accumulation of Knowledge: Pilgrimage as Leitmotif in the Indian Ocean in the Ancient Period', Frans Hüsken and Dick van der Meij, (eds.), *Reading*

Asia: New Research in Asian Studies, Richmond: Curzon Press, 2001: 110-127.

——, *The Archaeology of Seafaring in Ancient South Asia*, Cambridge World Archaeology Series, Cambridge: Cambridge University Press, 2003.

——, 'The Archaeology of Sacred Space: Introduction', in Ray, H.P. and Sinopoli, Carla (eds.), *Archaeology as History in Early South Asia*, New Delhi: Indian Council of Historical Research & Aryan Books International, 2004: 350-75.

——, 'From Multi-Religious Sites to Mono-religious monuments in South Asia: The Colonial Legacy of Heritage Management', Daly, Patrick and Winter, Tim, edited, *Routledge Handbook of Heritage in Asia*, London and New York: Routledge, 2012: 69-84.

Rhys Davids, T.W., 'Asoka and the Buddha-Relics', *Journal of the Royal Asiatic Society*, 1901: 397-410.

Sahu, N.K., *Buddhism in Orissa*, Cuttack: Utkal University, 1958.

Salomon, R., *Indian Epigraphy*, Austin: Center for Asian Studies, 1998.

Sarkar, H., *Studies in Early Buddhist Architecture of India*, New Delhi: Munshiram Manoharlal, 1993.

Sarkar, H. and Misra, B.N., *Nagarjunakonda*, New Delhi: Archaeological Survey of India, 1999.

Sarkar, H. and Nainar, S.P., *Amaravati*, New Delhi: Archaeological Survey of India, 1992.

Schopen, Gregory, 'Burial 'Ad Sanctos' and the Physical Presence of the Buddha in Early Indian Buddhism', *Religion*, 1987, 17: 193-225.

Schopen, Gregory, 'An Old Inscription from Amaravati and the Cult of the Local Monastic Dead in Indian Buddhist Monasteries', *Bones, Stones and Buddhist Monks*, Honolulu: University of Hawaii Press, 1997: chapter IX.

——, *Bones, Stones and Buddhist Monks*, Honolulu: University of Hawaii Press, 1997.

——, *Buddhist Monks and Business Matters*, University of Hawaii Press, 2004.

——, *Figments and Fragments of Mahayana Buddhism in India*, Honolulu: University of Hawaii Press, 2005.

Sinha, B.P. and S.R. Roy, *Vaisali Excavations 1958-62*, Patna: Directorate of Archaeology and Museums, Bihar, 1969.

Sircar, D.C., *Select Inscriptions Bearing on Indian History and Civilisation*, Calcutta: University of Calcutta, 1965.

——, *Inscriptions of Asoka*, third edition, New Delhi: Government of India, 1979.

Skilling, Peter, 'Cutting Across Categories: Relics in Pali Text', *Annual Report of the International Research Institute for Advanced Buddhology at Soka University,* 8, 2005: 269-332.

Spooner, D.B., 'Excavations at Shahji-ki-Dheri', *Annual Report of the Archaeological Survey of India*, 1908-9: 38-59.

Strong, John S., *The Legend of King Asoka, A Study and Translation of the Asokavadana*, Princeton: Princeton Library of Asian Translations, 1983.

Strong, John S., *Relics of the Buddha*, Princeton: Princeton University Press, 2004.

Suvorova, Anna A., *Muslim Saints of South Asia: The Eleventh to Fifteenth Centuries*, London: Routledge/Curzon, 2004.

Thapar, Romila, *Asoka and the Decline of the Mauryas*, New Delhi: Oxford India Paperbacks, 1998.

Trainor, Kevin, *Relics, Ritual and Representation in Buddhism*, Cambridge: Cambridge University Press, 1997.

Trivedi, P.K., *Further Excavations at Udayagiri – 2, Odisha*, New Delhi: Archaeological Survey of India, 2012.

Vogel, J. Ph., Buddhist Sculptures from Benares, *Archaeological Survey of India—Annual Report 1903-04,* Delhi: Swati Publications, 1990 (reprint).

Wagle, N., 1995, *Society at the Time of the Buddha*, Bombay: Popular Prakashan.

Walters, J.S., 'Stupa, Story and Empire: Constructions of the Buddha Biography in Early Post-Asokan India', Schober, J. ed., *Sacred Biography in the Buddhist Traditions of South and Southeast Asia*, Honolulu: University of Hawaii Press, 1997: 160-92.

Waterton, Emma and Smith, Laurajane (ed.), *Taking Archaeology Out of Heritage*, Cambridge Scholars Publishing, 2009.

Willis, M., *Buddhist Reliquaries from Ancient India*, London: The British Museum, 2000.

Wriggins, Sally Hovey, *The Silk Road Journey with Xuanzang*, Boulder: Westview Press, 2004.

Yamazaki, G., Kingship in Ancient India as Described in Literary Sources and Inscriptions', Karashima, N., (ed.), *Kingship in Indian History*, New Delhi: Manohar, 1999: 17-36.

Yamin, Mohammad, *Impact of Islam on Orissan Culture*, New Delhi: Readworthy Publications, 2009.

Yule, Paul, *Early Historic Sites in Orissa*, Delhi: Pragun Publication, 2006.

Yule, Paul, 'Early Forts in Eastern India', *Antiquity*, Vol. no. 082, Issue no. 316, June 2008.

Index